STUDENT COMPA
FOR

JULIA T. WOOD'S

COMMUNICATION MOSAICS:
An Introduction to the Field of Communication

Third Edition

Robert A. Cole
State University of New York Oswego

Clifford E. Kobland
State University of New York Oswego

Julia T. Wood
University of North Carolina-Chapel Hill

THOMSON
‐‐‐‐‐‐★‐‐‐‐ ™
WADSWORTH

Australia • Canada • Mexico • Singapore • South Africa • Spain • United Kingdom • United States

Cover image: Jose Ortega, *Una Raza, Un Mundo, Universo* (One Race, One World, One Universe) owned by MTA New York City Transit and comissioned by the Metropolitan Transit Authority. Photography © David Lubarsky

Printed in the United States of America
1 2 3 4 5 6 7 07 06 05 04 03

Printer: WestGroup

0-534-60735-7

For more information about our products, contact us at:
Thomson Learning Academic Resource Center
1-800-423-0563

For permission to use material from this text, contact us by:
Phone: 1-800-730-2214
Fax: 1-800-731-2215
Web: http://www.thomsonrights.com

Wadsworth/Thomson Learning
10 Davis Drive
Belmont, CA 94002-3098
USA

Asia
Thomson Learning
5 Shenton Way #01-01
UIC Building
Singapore 068808

Australia/New Zealand
Thomson Learning
102 Dodds Street
Southbank, Victoria 3006
Australia

Canada
Nelson
1120 Birchmount Road
Toronto, Ontario M1K 5G4
Canada

Europe/Middle East/South Africa
Thomson Learning
High Holborn House
50/51 Bedford Row
London WC1R 4LR
United Kingdom

Latin America
Thomson Learning
Seneca, 53
Colonia Polanco
11560 Mexico D.F.
Mexico

Spain/Portugal
Paraninfo
Calle/Magallanes, 25
28015 Madrid, Spain

CONTENTS

SECTION I

INTRODUCTION

This student companion is designed to assist you with your understanding and appreciation of the main textbook, *Communication Mosaics* Third Edition. First, we have provided a basic list of audiovisual resources that apply to textbook concepts and constructs. Next, you will find a writing guide and rough guide to citing resources. This is followed by instructions on how to do research through the Internet, how to use presentational software, and some general web resources for the communication course.

In Section II of the *Student Companion*, we provide outlines of the chapters in the textbook along with activities, journal items, panel ideas, discussion questions, and topical web resources. Section III contains self-test items and answers to go along with each chapter.

AUDIOVISUAL RESOURCES

Communication instructors often use feature films in their courses. Students who have been exposed to case studies/films often show higher levels of interest in the class and begin to apply communication concepts to both real and portrayed relationships. We have provided a list of potential feature films that correspond with concepts and constructs discussed in *Communication Mosaics*.

Feature Films With Strong Communication Themes

2003
All The Real Girls (2003). (personal relationships, conflict, nonverbal).

Bend It Like Beckham (2003). (perception, co-culture, adapting to diversity, verbal communication, personal identity, relationships).

The Pianist (2003). (conflict, co-cultures, intolerance, climates).

2002
8 Mile (2002). (co-cultures, adaptation to diversity, tolerance, conflict, mass media)

13 Conversations About One Thing (2003). (listening, personal identity, personal, personal relationships, self-disclosure).

About A Boy (2003). (self-identity, non-verbal, conflict).

Bowling For Columbine (2003). (communication climates, co-cultures, conflict, mass media).

Far From Heaven (2003). (personal identity, personal relationships, co-cultures, diversity, conflict,).

Monsoon Wedding (2003). (perception, adaptation, co-cultures, non-verbal, personal relationships,).

My Big Fat Greek Wedding (2003). (perception, co-cultures, adapting to diversity, groups).

2001
A Beautiful Mind (2003). (public communication, organizations, personal identity, personal relationships).

Almost Famous (2003). (mass communication, personal identity, personal relationships, media).

Bridget Jones's Diary (2003). (intrapersonal, personal identity, conflict, personal relationships).

Bully (2003). (groupthink, personal identity, conflict, groups).

Chicken Run (2003). (groups and teams, organizations, perception).

Crouching Tiger, Hidden Dragon (2003). (co-culture, non-verbal, adapting to diversity, personal relationships).

Ghost World (2003). (personal identity, verbal communication, perception,).

O (2003). (personal identity, personal relationships, intolerance, listening, teams, rites & rituals).

2000
Catfish in Black Bean Sauce (2000). (intercultural, co-culture, family, relational intimacy, relational stages).

Erin Brockovich (2000). (power, listening, nonverbal, self-disclosure, communication competence, persuasion, perception).

Hanging Up (2000). (intergenerational, family, listening, communication competence, perception).

Memento (2000). (personal identity, chronemics, listening).

Remembering the Titans (2000). (co-culture, prejudice, stereotypes, conflict, perception, power, self-disclosure).

What's Cooking (2000). (family, co-culture, listening, conflict, self-disclosure)

1999
Angela's Ashes (1999). (family, intergenerational, perception, prejudice, stereotypes, nonverbal, listening).

The Talented Mr. Ripley (1999). (communication competence, perception, self-disclosure, listening, nonverbal, gender, stereotypes).

The Straight Story (1999). (intergenerational, family, listening, perception, communication competence, emotion).

The Other Sister (1999). (perception, stereotypes, communication competence, family, prejudice, self-disclosure, listening).

The Green Mile (1999). (power, prejudice, stereotypes, perception, co-culture).

The End of the Affair (1999). (perception, nonverbal, relational intimacy, relational stages, listening, self-disclosure, gender).

The Cider House Rules (1999). (self-disclosure, perception, emotion, listening).

Snow Falling on Cedars (1999). (nonverbal, intercultural, stereotypes, prejudice, perception, relational intimacy, listening, communication competence).

Being John Malkovich (1999). (perception, nonverbal, relational intimacy, co-culture, gender, communication competence, listening).

American Beauty (1999). (intergenerational, self-perception, perception, family, communication climate, listening, co-culture, gender, relational stages).

1998
The Red Violin (1998). (listening, perception, conflict, relational stages, relational intimacy, family, stereotypes).

How Stella got her Groove Back (1998). (intergenerational, relational stages, relational intimacy, perception, co-culture, self-disclosure, listening).

Smoke Signals (1998). (relational stages, perception, intercultural, stereotypes, prejudice, self-disclosure, relational intimacy, listening, communication competence).

Shakespeare in Love (1998). (gender, nonverbal communication, perception, self-disclosure, communication competence).

High Art (1998). (emotion, perception, gender, co-culture, relational intimacy, self-disclosure).

A Bug's Life (1998). (group communication, listening, persuasion, communication climate, conformity, critical thinking, defiance, group roles, listening, perception, power).

Beloved (1998). (relational intimacy, perception, listening, relational stages, prejudice, stereotypes).

1997
Life is Beautiful/La Vita e Bella (1997). (family, prejudice, stereotypes, relational stages, relational intimacy, listening, intergenerational, communication competence).

Jerry McGuire (1997). (relational intimacy, communication climate, conflict).

In & Out (1997). (nonverbal, perception, stereotypes, co-culture, gender, prejudice, communication competence).

Chasing Amy (1997). (perception, gender, co-culture, relational intimacy, relational stages, stereotypes, self-disclosure).

1996
Truth about Cats and Dogs (1996). (self-concept, nonverbal, gender).

The American President (1996). (communication competence, perception).

Mr. Holland's Opus (1996). (communication climate, relational intimacy, self-concept).

Dead Man Walking (1996). (perception, stereotypes, prejudice, communication climate, listening, language).

Dangerous Minds (1996). (language, emotions, culture).

1995
Waiting to Exhale (1995). (friendship, listening, perception, nonverbal, relational intimacy, relational stages).

My Family (Mi Familia) (1995). (culture, communication climate, communication competence).

Grumpier Old Men (1995). (stereotypes, prejudice, perception, intergenerational, emotion, relational intimacy, relational stages, nonverbal, listening).

Clueless (1995). (language, culture, communication competence).

1994
Pulp Fiction (1994). (perception, language, relationships, listening, nonverbal, power, emotion).

Reality Bites (1994). (relational stages, self-disclosure).

Before Sunrise (1994). (nonverbal, relational stages, emotions).

1993
The Joy Luck Club (1993). (culture, communication competence, conflict).

Remains of the Day (1993). (nonverbal, relational intimacy, emotions).

Philadelphia (1993). (communication climate, perception, nonverbal).

Grumpy Old Men (1993). (stereotypes, prejudice, perception, intergenerational, emotion, relational intimacy, relational stages, nonverbal, listening).

1991
The Doctor (1991). (perception, empathy, roles).

Mississippi Masala (1991). (relational stages, perception, co-culture, intercultural, stereotypes, prejudice, self-disclosure, relational intimacy, listening, communication competence).

He Said, She Said (1991). (perception, gender, self-disclosure, relational intimacy, relational stages).

Boyz N the Hood (1991). (family communication, communication climate, conflict, self-concept).

1989
When Harry Met Sally (1989). (gender, relational stages).

Dead Poets Society (1989). (group communication, communication climate, conflict, critical thinking, defiance, group development, group polarization, self-concept).

1986
Children of a Lesser God (1986). (intercultural, communication climate, power, relational dialectics, relational stages).

1985
The Breakfast Club (1985). (group cohesiveness, group development, perception, power, roles, self-disclosure, status).

1983
Being There (1983). (language, perception).

1957
Twelve Angry Men (1957). (group communication, listening, persuasion, communication climate, conformity, critical thinking, defiance, group roles, listening, perception, power).

WRITING RESOURCES AND
ROUGH GUIDE TO CITING SOURCES

Writing Resources

Dictionary.com Writing Resources
http://dictionary.reference.com/writing/

The National Writing Project
http://www.writingproject.org/

You might try one of the Style Manuals and guidelines on-line

- **APA (American Psychological Association)**

    Citing Internet sources in APA:
    http://www.apa.org/journals/webref.html
    http://www.uvm.edu/~xli/reference/apa.html

- **MLA (Modern Language Association)**

    Citing Internet sources in MLA:
    http://www.uvm.edu/~xli/reference/mla.html

Style Guides

APA (American Psychological Association)
http://www.apastyle.org/elecref.html

MLA (Modern Language Association)
www.mla.org/

USING THE INTERNET FOR RESEARCH

The Internet can make research easy and even fun for you. Many of the following on-line sources allow you to view and even print full text articles and documents from the comforts of home.

Special Note: You should be educated about the general guidelines for evaluating information and research before you use these on-line sources for course projects. Sometimes there is just no substitute for a book or document that can only be found in the real library— and laziness is no excuse for sloppy research! However, on-line and Internet research sources can provide easily accessible information for your research.

Cyberlibraries
Cyber-library is the name for websites that are collections of typical public and university library materials. These libraries are accessible to users online—which means you don't have to physically go to the library! If you can access the Internet, you can use cyber-libraries. This technological option can be very useful as a quick way to find sources for presentations and other research projects.

Databases
Often found in cyberlibraries, databases are specialized collections of materials that share a common theme or academic interest. You can search an on-line database for research sources on your topic; most databases contain abstracts of the materials and some databases allow you to view and print full text articles from periodicals and academic journals. Some databases cover broad subject areas and some are very specialized. The following are resource links for libraries, databases, and other reference works to get you started:

Britannica
    http://www.britannica.com

Electronic Text Center at the University of Virginia Library
    http://etext.lib.virginia.edu/

Find Articles
    http://www.findarticles.com/PI/index.jhtml

Infoplease
    http://www.infoplease.com

Internet Public Library
    http://www.ipl.org/

Law Library of Congress

http://www.loc.gov/law/public/law.html

Library of Congress
http://www.loc.gov/

Lib-Web-Cats: A directory of Libraries Worldwide
http://www.librarytechnology.org/libwebcats/

Libweb: Library Servers via WWW
http://sunsite.berkeley.edu/Libweb/

National Archives
http://www.archives.gov/presidential_libraries/index.html

National Library of Medicine
http://www.nlm.nih.gov/

New York Public Library
http://www.nypl.org/

New York Public Library for the Performing Arts
http://www.nypl.org/research/lpa/lpa.html

Project Gutenberg
http://promo.net/pg/

Refdesk.com
http://www.refdesk.com

Schomburg Center for Research in Black Culture
http://www.nypl.org/research/sc/sc.html

UCLA Film & Television Library
http://www.cinema.ucla.edu/

Internet Search Engines
Search engines allow you to search the Internet for web pages and on-line documents
about your topic. Typically you can customize your search to limit the number of 'hits'
that are returned for your query. Or, to cover more Internet ground, you may want to use
a 'meta-search engine' which searches several resources at once. One of the biggest
pitfalls of using Internet search engines is that not all engines have records for all pages.
So, try your search using more than one engine. The website, 'Search Engine Watch'
(http://www.searchenginewatch.com/) is useful for learning about the capacities of
various search engines and how to use them effectively. Below is a collection of major
search engines, listed in approximate order of power and popularity.

Google
http://www.google.com

AllTheWeb.com
http://www.alltheweb.com

Yahoo
http://www.yahoo.com

MSN Search
http://search.msn.com

AOL Search
http://search.aol.com/

Ask Jeeves
http://www.askjeeves.com

HotBot
http://www.hotbot.com

Lycos
http://www.lycos.com

Specialty Search Engines
http://www.searchenginewatch.com

USING PRESENTATIONAL SOFTWARE

PowerPoint as Presentational Tool
It is likely that at some point in your college career, you will be called upon to make a class presentation. Using presentational software such as PowerPoint can be very useful for efficiently providing large quantities of information in a short period of time. Used appropriately, presentational software programs can generate a visual reinforcement of concepts and help your audience visualize relationships between ideas.

Despite its convenience and attractiveness, it is important to keep in mind that using PowerPoint presentations will significantly decrease the dialogue and interaction in your audience. When the lights go down, and the slide show comes on, people will diligently and busily write down anything that is on the screen (if they don't fall asleep first!). Particularly if there is too much information on the slides, audience members will be so busy writing that they won't listen to your presentation or respond to questions.

An option you can use to remedy this basic pitfall is to provide the audience a handout with PowerPoint slides on it, so that they can listen and respond rather than trying to write everything down. Furthermore, keep in mind that you will be fairly limited to using what you have previously entered on the slides— unlike a chalkboard, you can't easily erase things, add things, or draw arrows and such. You will be limited to a fairly linear presentation style that doesn't lend itself well to spontaneous adaptations or revisions.

PowerPoint as a Presentation Versus a Visual Aid for Presentations
PowerPoint is a useful means to provide dynamic and professional visual support to presentations. However, you need to understand the difference between a PowerPoint presentation/slide show and PowerPoint as a visual aid for presentations. Being clear about the difference will prevent you from giving your audiences very boring slide shows that do nothing more than click through a visual outline.

What is the difference between using PowerPoint as a presentation/slide show or a visual aid? Basically, a presentation stands alone and serves as the main source of information. It does not necessarily need a human narrator, and often it can be designed to run on its own from beginning to end. Presentations serve as the central foci rather than as supplemental materials for public communication and presentations tend to contain both written text and images, with little oral text.

A visual aid, however, is only a supplement to the presentation and speaker— it is not the main focus of the communication, nor is it the main source of information. Instead, the speaker and his or her words are the main focus. PowerPoint is used as a means to provide graphics, charts, statistics, pictures, and other visual aids common as public speaking supports. Visual aids, typically, are more image than text based, and they serve as a compliment, not a substitute, for the oral text. Hence, the speaker still has the fundamental responsibility to compose and deliver an effective oral text.

Audiences have pointed out several common problems as well as advantages when using PowerPoint. Here is a summary of their conclusions:

Problems using PowerPoint — What to avoid
1. Merely repeating your presentation or outlines on the slides is distracting and unnecessary.
2. Too much text is always bad, especially if it is a repetition of what you are saying. If you need to include text, use key words and phrases.
3. Sounds used for transitions and slide builds are unnecessary and distracting.
4. Excessive fonts, colors, images, and or background styles are overwhelming.
5. If you don't provide blank slides between your points, people get distracted looking at the slide and ignore the speaker. Too many slides are boring after a while.
6. Talking to the slides and not the audience limits eye contact.
7. Sometimes the equipment fails. If the presentation is totally dependent on the slides, then you're sunk.

Advantages to using PowerPoint — Why it is better than poster boards and overheads
1. You can provide colorful, easy to see graphics, charts, pictures, and comparisons.
2. It looks professional and credible, IF you use consistent fonts, colors, and backgrounds.
3. You can easily access or download things from the Internet to show the audience. This is easier and less expensive than trying to make color copies of books or pictures.
4. You can include video clips, pictures, and sound bites easily and this eliminates the need to have and to manage several different types of equipment (e.g. videotapes, tape recorders, easels, and overheads).
5. You can print paper handouts or make overhead transparencies from your slides to use as back-ups if the technology fails or as easy speaking notes.
6. It's much easier to carry across campus, and it doesn't get ruined when it rains!
7. You can attach PowerPoint slides to e-mail and share them, or post them to a website. This is useful for group presentations.

PowerPoint Resources:

Microsoft Office — PowerPoint Home Page
        http://www.microsoft.com/office/powerpoint/

Perspection Inc (Ed) (2001). *Microsoft PowerPoint Version 2002 Step by Step. Book & CD-ROM edition.* Microsoft Press. List Price: $29.99. Paperback: 352 pages. ISBN: 0735612978

Siegel, Kevin A. (2002). *Essentials of PowerPoint 2002 (XP)*. IconLogic. List Price: $35.00. Spiral-bound: 162 pages. ISBN: 1891762834

Wang, Wallace (2001). *Office XP For Dummies®.* John Wiley & Sons. List Price: $21.99. Paperback: 383 pages. ISBN: 076450830X

GENERAL INTERNET RESOURCES
FOR THE COMMUNICATION COURSE

Public Presentation Sources for Analysis/Criticism

Speech Bank
http://www.americanrhetoric.com/speechbank.htm

Top 100 U.S. Speeches
http://www.americanrhetoric.com/top100speeches.htm

Fallacies of Logic

LEO: Literacy Education Online Logical Fallacies
http://leo.stcloudstate.edu/acadwrite/logic.html

Taxonomy of Logical Fallacies
http://gncurtis.home.texas.net/taxonomy.html

National Communication Association Resources

Communication Careers
http://www.natcom.org/Instruction/Pathways/5thEd.htm

Expected Student Outcomes for Speaking and Listening
http://www.natcom.org/Instruction/Competencies/college_competencies.htm

NCA's Oral Communication Assessment Page
http://www.natcom.org/Instruction/assessment/Assessment/AssessMenu.htm

Service Learning
http://www.natcom.org/Instruction/sl/home.htm

Electronic Journals

American Communication Journal
http://www.acjournal.org/

CIOS/Communication Institute for Online Scholarship
http://www.cios.org/

Electronic Journal of Communication Research

http://www.cios.org/www/ejcmain.htm

The Edge: The E-Journal of Intercultural Relations
    http://www.interculturalrelations.com/

International Consortium for the Advancement of Academic Publications
    http://www.icaap.org/

Interpersonal Computing and Technology Journal
    http://jan.ucc.nau.edu/~ipct-j/index.html

Journal of Computer Mediated Communication
    http://jcmc.huji.ac.il/

Major Newspapers On-line

AllNewspapers.Com
    http://www.allnewspapers.com

100 Largest U.S. Newspapers
    http://www.freep.com/jobspage/links/top100.htm

Film & Television Guides

Internet Movie Database
    http://www.imdb.com/

In this section of the Student Companion you will find outlines for each of the chapters. To go along with each chapter, we have included learning activities, journal items, panel ideas, and questions for discussion. We have also included Internet resources related to each chapter's content.

Instructional Outlines

This section of the Student Companion provides concise summaries of each chapter's content. You probably read assigned chapters several days ahead of class lectures and weeks ahead of examinations. In such cases, it's possible to forget some of the topics covered in a chapter or to remember the content less clearly than is desirable. To assist you in recalling chapter material and to aid in reviewing for exams, the summaries in this section furnish brief outlines that are useful for identifying the author's main points and sub-points.

Learning Activities, Journal Items, Panel Items, Discussion Questions

In the pages that follow we suggest a variety of instructional resources to complement and extend coverage in the textbook. Each activity include here has been tested in our classes, and teachers and students alike have consistently judged them effective.

Using activities, films, journals, panels, and discussions is an excellent method for clarify and fortify the content of a course. **Activities** promote experiential learning by involving you in real or simulated communication situations in which you can practice, observe, and assess your communication skills. A good activity teaches principles and spurs your understanding of the conceptual bases of principles.

Journal Items are intended to generate greater awareness as you reflect on your own communication choices and behaviors, while observing the communication of those around you. It is important that the journal not become a personal diary. Instead, you should make direct connections to specific concepts from the course.

Panel Items can be used intermittently throughout the course, or might be assigned to you by the instructor in a more formal fashion. For example, (depending on class size, and time availability) you might be grouped with three or four other students and assigned the responsibility of organizing and moderating one of the panels. Such an assignment requires that you draw on a range on communication behaviors, including interpersonal, group, interviewing and presentational skills, along with research and organizational abilities.

Each chapter of the Student Companion also includes several **Discussion Questions**. Each question suggests how you might apply conceptual material to actual communication situations in your life.

Internet Web Page Resources
Included throughout the chapters are Internet web page URLs that can serve as additional resources for the topics. These websites provide an opportunity to explore in greater depth concepts that are raised by the author.

Chapter 1:
The Field of Communication

I.   There are many important reasons for studying communication.
- A. By learning about communication theories and principles you can become a more skilled communicator.
- B. By learning about communication theories and principles you can become more adept at making sense of what happens in your everyday life.

II.   Communication is a foundation of many spheres of life.
- A. Communication is a foundation in your personal life and identity.
    1. How we see ourselves reflects the views of us that are communicated by others.
    2. Healthy interactive communication influences our physical and psychological well-being.
- B. Communication is a foundation of the personal relationships that you develop with others.
    1. We connect with others by disclosing private information and solving problems together.
    2. Small talk and everyday communication weaves intimates' lives together.
- C. Communication is a foundation of your professional success.
    1. Communication skills are important for success and advancement in our professional careers.
    2. Technical careers also require good communication skills.
- D. Communication is a foundation of civic life and a healthy society.
    1. To participate in a democratic society we need to be able to listen, speak, and deliberate with others.
    2. Communication skills help us to interact with people whose background is different from our own.

III.   The study of communication has a long history.
- A. The study of communication dates back more than 2,500 years to ancient Greece.
    1. The philosophers Aristotle and Isocrates believed that rhetoric was essential to civic life.
    2. Aristotle wrote that persuasion occurs through the use of ethos, pathos and logos.
- B. In the 19th and early 20th Century, rhetoric was taught in Europe and the United State as part of a liberal arts education.
    1. Rhetoric was taught as the practical art of effective speaking.
    2. Communication professionals became interested in social issues and propaganda after the two world wars.
- C. Communication professionals began to use social scientific methods to research communication.

1. In the 1960s and 1970s communication professionals began to study interpersonal and group communication to understand how people interact.
        2. The field of communication continues to expand its topics and contexts of study.
    D. Since the 1970s communication professionals have been interested in the role of communication in social issues.
        1. A critical lens has been used to understand social and political movements.
        2. Scholars study who is allowed to communicate, who is not, and how this shapes cultures and societies.
    E. Studying communication prepares us to effectively participation in the world in which we live.

IV.   The study of communication is based on rigorous research.
    A. Communication scholars use quantitative research methods to gather information in numerical form.
        1. Descriptive statistics discuss human behavior in terms of quantity.
        2. Surveys are used to measure how people think, feel and act.
        3. Experiments are studies where the context is controlled by the researcher.
    B. Communication scholars use qualitative research methods to study how people interpret and give meaning to their experiences.
        1. Researchers interpret symbolic activity through textual analysis.
        2. Researchers conducting ethnographic studies immerse themselves in activities and contexts to gain insights and understanding.
        3. Qualitative scholars use historical research about significant past events, people, and activities.
    C. Communication scholars use critical research methods to identify and challenge communication practices that are harmful to individuals and social groups.
        1. Critical scholars want to use their research to promote social awareness.
        2. Some critical scholars develop new theories to help us understand how some groups and practices become dominant over others.

V.   Communication is a systemic process in which people interact with and through symbols to create and interpret meanings.
    A. Communication is a process. It is ongoing and always changing.
    B. Communication is systemic. It occurs within systems of interrelated and interacting parts.
    C. Communication is symbolic. Symbols are arbitrary, ambiguous, abstract representations of other things.

D. Communication involves meanings. Humans bestow significance on phenomena.
   1. Content level meanings are the literal meaning of messages.
   2. Relationship level meanings are what is expressed about the relationship between communicators in messages they send and receive.

VI. Models of Communication have offered increasingly sophisticated descriptions of what communication is and how it works.
   A. Simplistic linear models described communication as a one-way process in which one person (sender) affected another person (receiver).
   B. Interactive models described communication as interaction in which all parties participated actively in a sequence of sending and receiving messages and feedback.
   C. More sophisticated transactional models describe communication as a non-linear and not rigidly sequential activity in which each communicator is both a sender and a receiver and in which noise, systems, and time are influences.

VII. The modern field of communication includes ten areas of interest.
   A. Intrapersonal communication is communication with ourselves ('self-talk').
   B. Interpersonal communication focuses on communication between people, and it ranges from quite impersonal to highly interpersonal.
   C. Performance Studies examines how people's social, personal and professional identities and meanings of everyday life can be understood through performance.
   D. Group and team communication includes interaction in task, social, and personal groups and teams.
   E. Public communication includes both public speaking and criticism of public address.
   F. Organizational communication focuses on communication skills that affect work life and on organizational culture.
   G. Mass communication includes newspapers, television and movies, all of which shape and sometimes distort perceptions of people, events, and issues.
   H. Technologies of communication rely on electronic means of interaction. These technologies are revolutionizing how and with whom we communicate.
   I. Intercultural communication concentrates on how cultures shape individuals' ways of communicating and how, in turn, individuals' communication reflects and sometimes changes cultural values and understandings.
   J. Ethics and communication is a focus that infuses all the other areas in the field of communication.

VIII.   Different areas in the field of communication are unified by three central themes.
   A.   Symbolic activities are central to communication in contexts ranging from intrapersonal to intercultural.
   B.   Meanings are central to all forms of communication and meanings are created with symbols.
   C.   Ethics focuses on moral principles and codes of conduct.

IX.   Six processes are basic to communication of all types.
   A.   Communication requires us to perceive and understand ourselves, others, situations, and experiences.
   B.   The creation of communication climates creates a psychological environment for interaction.
   C.   Engaging in verbal communication is a second basic communication process.
   D.   Engaging in nonverbal communication is part of all interactions.
   E.   Communication requires listening and responding to others.
   F.   Adapting to contexts and others is basic to communication of all sorts.

X.   The study of communication opens doors to a wide array of careers.
   A.   Research, both academic and for media companies, is a career option for communication specialists.
   B.   Communication education at all levels is an exciting career for people who want to help others improve their communication skills.
   C.   Careers in mass communication range from script writing and directing to reporting.
   D.   The field of training and consulting welcomes individuals with strong backgrounds in communication.
   E.   Human relations and management is a career that places a high priority on communication knowledge and applications.

Vocabulary Terms

Communication

Communication climate

Content/Relational levels of meaning

Critical research methods

Ethics

Fantasy theme

Feedback

Interactive model of communication

Interpersonal communication

Intrapersonal communication

Linear/Actional/Transactional models of communication

Listening

Meaning

Noise

Organizational culture

Perceptions

Performance Studies

Process

Qualitative/Quantitative research methods

Symbols

System(s)

ACTIVITY 1.1: What Do You Think About Communication?

Purpose/Objective:
This exercise will allow you consider what your understanding of communication is, prior to having taken this class and to see if your understanding has changed by the end of the course.

Instructions:
Below is a list of statements about communication. Read each statement and then mark the answer that best fits your understanding as you begin the course. Return to this list during the final weeks of the course and see if any of your responses have changed.

Rating Scale: 1= Always True   3= Mostly False
                 2= Mostly True   4= Always False

View at start of course	View at end of course	
____	____	1. The biggest obstacle faced by people in long-distance relationships is that they cannot share the 'big' moments with each other.
____	____	2. Sometimes we simply choose not to hear what it is that others have to say.
____	____	3. A good dictionary like the *Oxford English Dictionary* is the final source for clarifying what a word really means.
____	____	4. While nonverbal communication is valuable, verbal communication is more important.
____	____	5. We are pretty much born the way we are, with very little chance of making major changes to our personality.
____	____	6. 'Men are from Mars and Women are from Venus' when it comes to communicating with each other.
____	____	7. It is the speaker who is responsible for a message's effects and for clarifying any miscommunication.
____	____	8. One sign of a close relationship is that the people are able to avoid conflict.
____	____	9. In the United States there is one main culture and quite a few subordinate cultures.
____	____	10. Sometimes we decide that we are intentionally going to not communicate with others.
____	____	11. The best communicators have worked hard to eliminate all anxiety about communicating. Natural born communicators are lucky enough to not experience anxiety.
____	____	12. For groups to be effective, someone needs to take charge and direct others.

ACTIVITY 1.2: The Classroom Model

Purpose/Objective:
This exercise will help you understand the various models of communicating by applying them to the classroom you are in.

Instructions:
Review the textbook's discussion of the models of communication. Reflecting on your own Communication classroom, build a model that identifies senders, receivers, messages, noise, feedback, channels, fields of experience, time, etc.

Would you say that your Communication class more closely approximates a Linear, Interactive, or Transactional model of communication?

ACTIVITY 1.3: Establishing Study Skills—Flash Cards

Purpose/Objective:
This activity will help you absorb and integrate the course concepts into your life, and assist you in reviewing for examinations.

Instructions:
At the start of each chapter, create a set of flash cards. On 3'x5' index cards, write the list of vocabulary terms, provided in your *Student Companion*. On the reverse side of each card, write a definition of the term and give an example of the concept in practice.

At the conclusion of each chapter, drill yourself on the vocabulary terms. In preparation for exams, review the vocabulary terms to ensure that you understand the concepts of the chapter.

ACTIVITY 1.4: Establishing Study Skills—Crossword Puzzle

Purpose/Objective:
This activity will help you absorb and integrate the course concepts into your life, and assist you in reviewing for examinations.

Instructions:
At the conclusion of each chapter, create a crossword puzzle that contains the vocabulary terms provided in your *Student Companion*. Build a list of clues based on the definitions for the vocabulary terms.

Locate a classmate, or classmates, who are willing to build their own crossword puzzles for each chapter. Exchange puzzles with each other as a way to test your recall of the chapter's concepts. In preparation for exams, each of you should build more elaborate crossword puzzles that draw on the range of concepts that will be tested.

ACTIVITY 1.5: Establishing Study Skills—Communication for $100

Purpose/Objective:
This activity will help you absorb and integrate the course concepts into your life, and assist you in reviewing for examinations.

Instructions:
Locate two or more classmates who are interested in reviewing the course concepts and building a *Jeopardy* game to test your knowledge about communication.

Assign one or more categories to each person corresponding to each chapter in the textbook. For example, the categories would be 'Perception,' Listening,' 'Nonverbal Communication,' etc. Using the vocabulary items provided in the *Student Companion*, questions should be developed that relate to each category.

Once everyone has his or her questions prepared, ask someone to moderate the game. Play should following the format used on the game show, *Jeopardy*. However, players should not answer questions categories for which they were assigned to develop questions.

ACTIVITY 1.6: Media Watch—What Makes Them So Good?

Purpose/Objective:
This exercise should provide an opportunity to analyze communicators in the mass media to determine what makes them so good at what they do.

Instructions:
Select your favorite communicator from among the following mass media:

Musical recording artist
Film or television actor/actress
Television news/sports/weathercaster
Radio announcer
Newspaper/newsmagazine columnist

For each person you select, list three characteristics that make them stand out as communicators. Reflect on how they are able to develop a personalized relationship with their listeners/readers. In your opinion, which model best describes the communication that occurs between the media personality and her or his followers?

JOURNAL ITEMS

1. Describe and analyze a communication situation in which you were aware of making an ethical choice. How did you decide what kind of communication was ethical? Can you use your criterion (or criteria) as a general standard or guide for ethical communication?

2. Review the text's discussion of different areas in the field of communication. Identify the kinds of communication in which you are most and least effective. Select one area in which you will work for immediate improvement and another area for long-term improvement.

PANEL IDEAS

1. Because this chapter will probably be presented at the start of the course, it may be too soon for students to organize a panel. Perhaps, introduce the idea of communication panels as an ongoing feature of the course, and if they are to be a regular assignment, select which students will be responsible for facilitating which topics during the course.

DISCUSSION QUESTIONS

1. Using each of the models discussed in this chapter, describe interaction and transaction as depicted in feature films, Internet, or fictional books. What does each model highlight or obscure? Which model better describes and explains communication in the selected context?

2. Break into small groups. Provide three examples or scenarios where you can identify both the content and the relationship level of meaning. Prepare a brief, informal presentation to the class.

INTERNET WEB PAGE RESOURCES

Center for Communication
http://www.cencom.org/

Communication Institute for Online Scholarship
http://www.cios.org

Communication Library Resource Guide
http://www.west.asu.edu/lehnerj/Comm_guide.htm

Electronic Journal of Communication
http://www.cios.org/www/ejcmain.htm

International Communication Association
http://www.icahdq.org/

Journal of Mass Media Ethics
http://jmme.byu.edu

Journalism Resources
http://bailiwick.lib.uiowa.edu/journalism/

Mind, Culture and Activity Homepage
http://www.communication.ucsd.edu/MCA/

National Communication Association
http://www.natcom.org

Toastmasters International
http://www.toastmasters.org/

Chapter 2:
Perceiving and Understanding

I.   Perception is an active, three-part, interrelated process of selecting, organizing and interpreting phenomena.

    A. Selection is the process of choosing which aspects of reality to notice.

        1. We notice things that stand out because they are intense, large, or unusual.

        2. We can talk to ourselves to influence what we selective attend to.

        3. Our needs, interests and motives also influence what we selectively perceive.

    B. Organization occurs when we use cognitive schemata to arrange perceptions in meaningful ways.

        1. Prototypes define the clearest, most representative examples of categories.

        2. Personal constructs are bi-polar dimensions of judgment we use to assess phenomena.

        3. Stereotypes are predictive generalizations about phenomena.

        4. Scripts are action guides that reflect our expectations of how we, and others, will behave in specific situations.

    C. Interpretation is the subjective process of creating explanations for what we observe and experience.

        1. Attributions are explanations of why things happen or why people act as they do.

            a. Dimensions of attributions are internal or external locus; stability; and controllability.

        2. Self-serving bias occurs when attributions serve the self-interests of the person constructing the attribution.

        3. Attributions are subjective; they are not factual explanations of others' behavior.

II.   Perception is influenced by many factors.

    A. Physiological factors shape perceptions.

        1. The five senses affect perceptions.

        2. Stress, illness, fatigue and biorhythms also determine perceptions.

        3. Factors such as age and gender can also influence perceptions.

    B. Expectations influence perceptions.

        1. Perceptions may be affected by exposure to words that make something salient.

        2. Positive visualization is effective in reducing communication apprehension.

    C. Cognitive abilities affect how and what we perceive.

1. Cognitive complexity refers to the number of constructs used, how abstract they are, and how elaborately they interact in our efforts to interpret phenomena.
            2. Person-centeredness is the ability to perceive and act toward another as a unique individual.
            3. Empathy refers to the ability to feel what another person feels in a situation.
   D. Social roles shape our perceptions.
            1. Training for a role and its demands influences interpretations.
   E. Cultural factors influence perceptions.
            1. A culture consists of beliefs, values, understandings and ways of interpreting experience that a number of people share.
            2. Western culture emphasizes speed while some other countries prefer a more leisurely pace.

III.   Four guidelines can improve skills in perceiving.
   A. Avoid mind reading.
            1. Do not assume you understand what another person thinks or feels.
   B. Check perceptions with others.
            1. Compare subjective perceptions to arrive at common understandings.
   C. Distinguish facts from inferences.
            1. Use tentative words to avoid mistakenly going beyond the facts.
   D. Monitor the self-serving bias.
            1. Avoid blaming others or judging them too harshly.

Vocabulary Terms

Attribution

Cognitive complexity

Cognitive schemata

Constructivism

Controllability

Culture

Empathy

Facts

Individualism

Inference

Interpretation

Internal/External locus

Mind reading

Monitoring

Perception

Personal Constructs

Person-centeredness

Positive Visualization

Prototypes

Schemata

Scripts

Self-serving bias

Stability

Stereotypes

ACTIVITY 2.1: Create Your Own First Impression

Purpose/Objective:
This activity will provide insight into the ways by which we present ourselves to others.

Instructions:
Because people quickly form impressions of others, it is a good idea to plan ahead for the kind of first impression you would like to make. What images of yourself would you like to project? Exactly what impression would you like to make?

List aspects of your self-image:

1.

2.

3.

Next, identify those nonverbal strategies that you can use to stimulate those images you listed above. What nonverbal behaviors, clothing, or artifacts would you use to accomplish those first impressions with your audience?

List of nonverbal behaviors

1.

2.

3.

Finally, identify verbal strategies that you can use to initiate a positive first impression.

List of verbal behaviors

1.

2.

3.

ACTIVITY 2.2: Selective Perception

Purpose/Objective:
This activity is designed to make you aware of how we selectively perceive the world and how much 'raw reality' we usually do not notice.

Instructions:
Try to perceive the environment around you more fully than you usually do by concentrating on each of your five senses. Write down as much as you can in an effort to capture the stimuli that you perceive.

Begin with vision. Describe what you see in the room. After they've identified obvious visual aspects of the room, push yourself to be more observant. Perhaps the paint is chipped, there is a scene outside that can be viewed through the window, the light in the room has a yellow tone, the fluorescent light is flickering, and so forth.

Next, close your eyes and focus on what you can hear in the room. After considering the obvious auditory stimuli, focus more closely and notice other sounds: a bird singing, noise in the hallway, breathing of other people, and so forth. Follow this procedure for the senses of touch, smell, and taste.

At the conclusion, review your list and reflect on how this exercise illustrates the process of perception. Consider why you didn't initially perceive all of the stimuli that you were eventually able to notice using each sense. What factors influenced what you most readily perceived.

ACTIVITY 2.3: How I See You

Purpose/Objective:
The purpose of this activity is to provide you with a concrete understanding of how you use cognitive schemata to organize your perceptions of others.

Instructions:
Review the textbook's discussion of the four kinds of cognitive schemata: prototypes, constructs, stereotypes, and scripts. Write a paragraph for each of the schemata applying your perceptions of the course instructor.

Examples of prototypes of the course instructor might be liberal, teacher, woman. Constructs might include intelligent-unintelligent, funny-not funny, attractive-unattractive, personal-impersonal. Examples of stereotypes might include expectations that students do the readings, is open to conversations outside of class. Last, scripts for the instructor could be that it is appropriate to challenge or disagree with this professor, you are required to respect what others say in the class, and so forth.

Review what you've written about the course instructor. This is your active construction of the perception of someone else. Ask yourself if you have constructed your perceptions in an ethical, responsible manner. Are there aspects of the instructor you may have misconstrued?

Put these perceptions of the instructor away for a month or two, and then reread what you wrote. How accurate were your perceptions? What aspects would you now change?

ACTIVITY 2.4: What's My Role?

Purpose/Objective:
This exercise will clarify how different roles people hold shape their perceptions of the world.

Instructions:
For each of the roles listed below, describe in a couple of sentences how they might perceive the following:

A large forest on the outskirts of a metropolitan area.
A logger

An environmentalist

A city planner

A boy scout

A hunter

A full moon
An astronomer

Two lovers

A lost hiker

A child who has read about werewolves

 A sailor

A fast, expensive, new sports car
An 18-year-old youth

The parents of an 18-year-old youth

A local traffic officer

An insurance agent

ACTIVITY 2.5: Young, Old, Rich, Poor, Fast, Slow

Purpose/Objective:
This exercise is designed to allow you to hear how people from other cultures perceive the world differently.

Instructions:
Arrange to speak to people from countries and cultures different than yours. You might wish to use the Internet and message software or discussion boards to complete this activity.

Locate people who are willing to share their cultural perceptions on the topics listed below. Makes notes of their answers and reflect on how culture attitudes shape individuals' perceptions of life.

Age

Individualism

Wealth

Pace (time)

Technology

Medicine

Government

ACTIVITY 2.6: Media Watch—That's Horrible

Purpose/Objective:
This activity will give you a better understanding of how perceptions can be intentionally manipulated.

Instructions:
Rent a horror movie from the local video store. Pay particular attention to how the film's director uses the environment, music, camera angles, dialogue, and so forth to create tension and suspense.

Also examine how the viewer's perceptions of the characters are orchestrated by the director. For example, how do we know who is good and who is bad? What cultural cues are embedded in films from the horror genre that signal what we are supposed to think and feel? What prototypes, constructs, stereotypes, and scripts are evident in the film?

JOURNAL ITEMS

1. Describe your schemata for close friends. Who is your prototype? What constructs are primary in your thinking about friends? What stereotypes do you have for friends? What scripts describe interaction with friends?

2. Analyze the attributional patterns you use to explain a mean or disappointing behavior by a good friend and by someone who you do not like. Analyze how differences in your feelings about the two individuals affect your attributional tendencies.

PANEL IDEA

1. Multi-racial Panel: Create a panel of individuals who are of different non-Caucasian races that are substantially represented on your campus (I generally invite an American Indian, an African American, a Latino or Latina, and an Asian American). In this case it would be ideal to have panelists who are students so that they can talk peer-to-peer with members of your class.

   Set the tone for open, candid discussion by reminding the class that there are many communication challenges and difficulties among the different races in our society. Explain that this panel is an opportunity for people to talk openly about communication barriers between races. After introducing the panelists to your class, invite each of them to make an opening statement of 3- 5 minutes about communication problems they experience on the campus. After all panelists have made general statements, invite questions from the class. Facilitate discussion to make sure that it remains constructive and focused on how our differing perceptions influence our interpretations. Also remind students of the importance of perception checks.

DISCUSSION QUESTIONS

1. Prior to class, spend about 15 to 20 minutes in an online chat room of their choice. During class time, break into groups to discuss/apply key terms from the chapter to what they discovered in the chat room. Pay particular attention to how you perceived others and they perceived you. How accurately do you suppose people presented themselves?

2. Reflect on how you have changed over your lifetime. Did others perceive those differences? Why or why not? Think about someone you've known for a long time. In what ways have you changed your perceptions of them? What about someone you met who made a strong first impression on you. After you got to know them better, were your perceptions of them altered? Why or why not? Can

you think of someone you started out not liking but then liked later? How about the other way around. How do you explain this?

INTERNET WEB PAGE RESOURCES

AARP
>http://www.aarp.org/

Gerontological Society of America
>http://www.geron.org/

Journal of Experimental Psychology
>http://www.apa.org/journals/xhp.html

Journal of Social and Personal Relationships
>http://www.jspr.org

Media & Perception
>http://www.thirteen.org/edonline/lessons/media/b.html

Optical Illusions
>http://www.optillusions.com/

Senses in Human Communication
>http://www.law.pitt.edu/hibbitts/senses.htm

Chapter 3:
Creating Communication Climates

I.   Communication climate is the overall emotional tone of people interacting in a relationship.
   - A. Creating constructive communicative climates influence the effectiveness of communication in all contexts.
   - B. Communication climates are basic to all settings and forms of interaction.

II.   Communication climate is strongly influenced by the extent to which people feel confirmed or disconfirmed.
   - A. Recognition is the most basic type of confirmation.
       1. Recognition is communicated by verbal and/or nonverbal behaviors that affirm that a person exists.
       2. Lack of recognition is communicated by verbal and/or nonverbal behaviors that ignore a person's presence.
   - B. Acknowledgment is a second, more powerful, level of confirmation.
       1. Acknowledgment is communicated by verbal and/or nonverbal behaviors that convey a person matters and is heard.
       2. Lack of acknowledgment is communicated by verbal and/or nonverbal behaviors that disconfirm what a person thinks and/or feels.
   - C. Endorsement is the highest level of confirmation.
       1. Endorsement is communicated by verbal and/or nonverbal behaviors that convey acceptance of what another feels and/or thinks.
       2. Lack of endorsement is communicated by verbal and/or nonverbal behaviors that deny or disapprove what a person thinks and/or feels.
       3. Endorsement is not necessarily agreement, nor does disconfirmation necessarily mean disagreement.

III.   Specific kinds of communication can foster either defensive or supportive communication climates.
   - A. Descriptive communication fosters a more supportive climate than evaluative communication.
       1. We tend to feel defensive when others evaluate us.
       2. Descriptive communication describes without passing judgment.
   - B. Provisional communication fosters a more supportive climate than certainty communication.
       1. Certainty suggests there is one valid answer, point of view, or course of action.
       2. Ethnocentrism, a form of certainty communication, is the assumption that our culture and its norms are the only right ones.

3. Provisionalism, an alternative to certainty, signals an openness, a willingness to accept other viewpoints

C. Spontaneous communication, which is more open and non-manipulative, fosters a more supportive climate than strategic communication that aims to manipulate by keeping motives and intentions hidden.

D. Problem-oriented communication, which focuses on resolving tensions and problems, fosters a more supportive climate than controlling communication that attempts to dominate.

E. Empathic communication, which confirms the worth and concern of others, fosters a more supportive climate than neutral communication that implies indifference.

F. Communication that expresses equality fosters an open climate through which interaction flows freely while communication that expresses superiority creates a sense of defensiveness.

IV. Conflict exists when individuals who depend on each other have different views, interests, or goals and perceive their differences as incompatible.

A. Conflict is probably inevitable in all relationships.
   1. Conflict is a sign that individuals are involved and interdependent.
   2. Conflict does not necessarily indicate that a relationship is in trouble.
   3. For the most part we have conflict only with people who matter to us.

B. Conflict may be overt or covert.
   1. Overt conflict exists when individuals express differences openly and straightforwardly.
   2. Covert conflict exists when people camouflage disagreement, or deny differences, and express them indirectly.
   3. Covert conflict is less constructive and less open to resolution than overt conflict.

C. Conflict can be managed well or poorly.
   1. People responding to conflict reflect one of three distinct orientations: lose-lose, win-lose, and win-win.
      a. The lose-lose approach assumes that conflict results in losses for everyone.
      b. The win-lose approach assumes that one person wins and the other loses.
      c. The win-win approach assumes that there are usually ways to resolve differences so that everyone wins.
   2. There are four responses to conflict: exit, neglect, loyalty, and voice.
      a. Exit responses, which involves leaving relationships either physically or psychologically, are active and can be destructive.

     b. Neglect responses, which occurs when one denies or minimizes the problem, are passive and can be destructive.

     c. Loyalty responses, which involve staying committed despite differences, are passive and can be constructive.

     d. Voice responses, which attempts to resolve problems, are active and constructive.

  D. Conflict when managed constructively can be beneficial to relationships.

    1. Conflict can stimulate individual growth.

    2. Conflict can strengthen relationships.

    3. Conflict can deepen insight into our own thoughts and feelings.

    4. Conflict allows us to consider points of view that differ from our own.

V. Five guidelines can help us build and sustain healthy communication climates.

  A. Accept and confirm others giving friends honest feedback even if it isn't always pleasant.

  B. Affirm and assert yourself, communicating your thoughts and feelings that allow others the opportunity to confirm you.

  C. Respect diversity among people for it is usually counterproductive to try to form all people and relationships into a single mode.

  D. Time your conflict effectively.

    1. Try to engage in conflict when both people are able to be fully present and mindful.

    2. Be flexible.

    3. Bracket time to mark off peripheral issues for later discussion.

  E. Show grace, a willingness to forgive and put aside our needs to help others, when appropriate.

Vocabulary Terms

Acknowledgment

Bracketing

Communication climate

Confirmation

Conflict

Covert conflict

Empathy

Endorsement

Ethnocentrism

Grace

Lose-lose

Overt conflict

Provisionalism

Recognition

Win-lose

Win-win

ACTIVITY 3.1: Recognize, Acknowledge, Endorse

Purpose/Objective:
To better understand the difference in attitudes and behaviors associated with various levels of confirmation and disconfirmation.

Instructions:
Listed below are two cases in which people might find themselves in strong disagreement. Imagine that you have an opportunity to share your views with others. Prepare three 1-minute opening statements for each case that exhibit, recognition, acknowledgement, and endorsement for your opponent.

Case 1) You are a logger whose livelihood depends on your ability to harvest trees from the nearby forests. You are at the town hall meeting to speak out against a proposal by local environmentalist who seek to prohibit all harvesting of timber. Write an opening to your statement that, even though you are in disagreement with them, demonstrates:

a) Recognition and confirmation of your opponent.

b) Acknowledgement and confirmation of your opponent.

c) Endorsement and confirmation of your opponent.

Case 2) You believe animals should not be harmed, no matter what the reason and you wish to speak out against animal research in a letter to the editor. Write an opening to your statement that, even though you are in disagreement with them, demonstrates:

a) Recognition and confirmation of your opponent.

b) Acknowledgement and confirmation of your opponent.

c) Endorsement and confirmation of your opponent.

ACTIVITY 3.2: Creating Supportive Communication Climates

Purpose/Objective:
To practice communicating in a way that creates a supportive climate.

Instructions:
Following each statement below, write out responses that foster a supportive interpersonal climate. Your responses should follow the directions given.

Example:
Statement: I should have studied harder for the test.
Response: (descriptive) You don't think you studied enough.
Response: (empathic) I know how you feel.

_____

Statement 1: I think Pat is cheating on me.

Response: (provisionalism) _____

_____

Response: (problem-orientation) _____

_____

Response: (description) _____

_____

Statement 2: I think I need to go on a diet.

Response: (empathy)_____

_____

Response: (provisionalism) _____

_____

Response: (equality) _____

_____

Statement 3: Do you think it's ever right to tell a lie?

Response: (spontaneity) _____

_____

Response: (provisionalism) _____

_____

Response: (equality) _____

_____

Statement 4: My counselor suggested that I go on medication to control my depression.

Response: (problem-orientation) _____

_____

Response: (description) _____

_____

Response: (equality) _____

_____

ACTIVITY 3.3: Communication Confirmation

Purpose/Objective:
This activity should help you develop communication responses that promote various levels of confirmation in others.

Instructions:
If you do not recall the textbook's discussion of levels of confirmation and the communication that creates them, then reread the discussion.

Listed below are four situations. For each one, write a statement that expresses each of the three levels of confirmation: recognition, acknowledgment, and endorsement. Use parentheses to indicate nonverbal communication of each level of confirmation.

Example:
A two-year -old child runs up to you and says, 'Look, look, I found a four leaf clover.'

A. recognition:	Hello. (Smile)
B. acknowledgement:	So you're pretty excited, aren't you?
C. endorsement:	Wow! You're right. You did find a four leaf clover.

1. Your best friend comes to your place without having mentioned she/he was coming by. Your friend walks in and says, 'I'm really worried about what's happening between my parents. They seem angry with each other all the time lately, and I think they may be thinking about a separation or divorce.'

A. recognition:

B. acknowledgment:

C. endorsement:

2. At a meeting of a political group, someone whom you know only casually says to you, 'All we ever do in this group is talk. We never really DO anything. I am very frustrated by the lack of action.'

A. recognition:

B. acknowledgment:

C. endorsement:

3. While you are home over break, one of your parents says to you, 'I'm worried about your uncle. His health is failing, and I think maybe we need to move him into a nursing home.'

A. recognition:

B. acknowledgment:

C. endorsement:

4. The person whom you have been dating steadily for 4 months tells you, 'I don't like the way we handle conflict. Whenever we disagree about something, it seems that each of us digs our heels in and refuses to listen to the other or to even try to understand the other's point of view.'

A. recognition:

B. acknowledgment:

C. endorsement:

ACTIVITY 3.4: Styles for Responding to Conflict

Purpose/Objective:
This activity will help you identify you preferred style(s) for responding to conflicts.

Instructions:
Indicate how you would be likely to respond to the five scenarios presented on the following two pages.

Afterward, check you score against the exit-voice-loyalty-neglect model of responses to conflict. If you not satisfied with your style, remember that changing an undesirable way of responding to conflict is possible. Begin by monitoring yourself in conflict situations and then experimenting with responses other than your habitual ones.

Read the five scenarios below. For each one, indicate which of the four possible responses you think it is most likely you would follow.

To score your conflict response inventory, turn to the key on the page following the inventory.

1. The person that you have been dating for six months tells you that she/he is upset by your lack of interest in spending time with her/his friends. You don't want to spend time with your partner's friends, but she/he sees this as an issue that the two of you need to resolve. In this situation, you would be most likely to:

A. Walk out on the conversation
B. Tell her/him that the issue isn't important
C. Say nothing and hope the issue will go away
D. Actively work to find a resolution that satisfies both of you.

2. Last week a friend let you use his/her computer when yours crashed. Accidentally, you erased a couple of files on your friend's computer. Later, the friend confronts you about the erased files and the friend seems really angry. In this situation, you would be most likely to:

A. Tune out your friend's criticism and anger.
B. Agree that you had made an error and ask how you could make it up to your friend.
C. Say nothing and hope your friend's anger blows over and the friendship continues.
D. Tell your friend that it's not a big deal since he/she always backs up the hard disk on diskettes.

3. Your roommate tells you that you are a slob and that she/he wants the two of you to agree to some ground rules about cleaning and putting things up. In this situation, you would be most likely to:

A. Agree to be neater, even though you don't think it's fair that you should have to operate by your roommate's standards.
B. Tell your roommate that cleaning is not a big deal in the big picture of living together.
C. Agree that the two of you differ in how you like the place to look and offer to work out some mutually acceptable rules.
D. Leave the situation and hope that your roommate will let the matter drop.

4. The person you have been dating for a while says that you are too critical and too negative, and she/he says she/he wants you to work on changing that aspect of your behavior. Although you realize this may be a fair criticism of you, you find it uncomfortable to hear.   Further, you have no idea how you could eliminate or improve your tendency to be judgmental. In this situation, you would be most likely to:

A. Agree with your dating partner's perceptions and ask if she/he has any suggestions for how you might reduce your critical, negative tendencies.
B. Shrug and ignore the criticism.
C. Say nothing and hope things get better.
D. Point out that being critical is not really a major issue in whether two people are compatible.

5. Your parents call you to criticize you for not staying in touch. They say they want you to come home more often and call a couple of times each week. You are very involved in the campus scene and don't want to be running home all the time. In this situation, you would be most likely to:

A. Tell your parents they are creating a problem when none really exists
B. Agree that you haven't stayed in touch and promise to be better in the future; then follow through on your promise even though it isn't your preference.
C. Tell your parents that you want to work with them to come up with ways you can stay in better touch without separating you from the campus too much.
D. Ignore their phone calls and e-mails, figuring you'll see them during the term break and get it resolved then.

Scoring the Conflict Response Inventory

The four choices for your action in each scenario represent the responses of exit, voice, loyalty, and neglect.

Scoring:

	Exit	Voice	Loyalty	Neglect
1.	A	D	C	B
2.	A	B	C	D
3.	D	C	A	B
4.	B	A	C	D
5.	D	C	B	A

Questions to consider in interpreting your scores:

1. Did you rely on a single response in three or more of the situations?

2. Did you rely more on exit and neglect (combined) than on voice and loyalty (combined)?

3. What are the advantages and disadvantages of your response style(s)?

ACTIVITY 3.5: Alternate Ways of Responding to Conflict

Purpose/Objective:
This activity will give you practice in generating communication that reflects each of the four responses to interpersonal conflict. The exercise should increase your repertoire of methods for responding to interpersonal conflict.

Instructions:
If you do not recall the textbook's discussion of different responses to conflict, review that section of the chapter.

Listed below are five conflict scenarios. For each one, write four responses—one each that reflects exit, voice, loyalty, and neglect responses.

Scenario 1

The person you have been dating suggests that it's time the two of you talked about commitment. You feel unready to discuss a serious relationship, but your partner insists that she/he thinks the two of you need to talk about it.

A. exit response:

B. voice response:

C. loyalty response:

D. neglect response:

Scenario 2

One of your friends brings up a political race, and you make a comment about the strengths of the candidate you support. Your friend says, 'I can't believe you support that jerk. What has he done for the environment?'

A. exit response:

B. voice response:

C. loyalty response:

D. neglect response:

Scenario 3

One of your co-workers continuously misses deadlines in turning in reports to you. Since your reports require information from the co-worker's reports, your reports also are late. You don't want your late reports to interfere with your raises and advancement. You'd like for the co-worker to be more prompt.

A. exit response:

B. voice response:

C. loyalty response:

D. neglect response:

Scenario 4

You tell your parents you'd like to take a term off from school. They are strongly opposed to the idea and they tell you to stay in school.

A. exit response:

B. voice response:

C. loyalty response:

D. neglect response:

Scenario 5

You and your friend generally get together to watch the playoffs at his apartment. This year, your friend suggests that the two of you go downtown to one of the bars that has a giant screen. Where you watch doesn't really matter to you.

A. exit response:

B. voice response:

C. loyalty response:

D. neglect response:

ACTIVITY 3.6: Media Watch—Win/Lose

Purpose/Objective:
To gain a better understanding of how the news media frame issues of disagreement among nations.

Instructions:
Read the news stories associated with three or four different international conflicts. For example, find stories related to trouble in the Middle East, the conflict in Northern Ireland, fighting among African nations, or strife among Baltic nations.

Use a variety of media such as newspapers like the *New York Times*, newsmagazines like *Newsweek* and *U.S. News & World Report*, television networks like CBS or CNN, and radio networks like Nation Public Radio and the BBC.

As you read the stories, try to determine if they cast the disagreements in terms of Win-Lose, Lose-Lose, or Win-Win. Consider what the implications are when media frame readers' understandings of these conflicts in those terms.

JOURNAL ITEMS

1. Identify one relationship in which you generally feel supported and comfortable. Identify a second relationship in which you usually or frequently feel defensive and on-guard. Describe the communication in these two relationships. How does it differ? How does the communication in each relationship reflect what you read about communication climates?

2. Most of us learn responses to conflict from observing others, especially members of our families of origins. Reflect on your family and the ways of responding to conflict used by your parents and siblings. Describe those patterns. To what extent do your habitual ways of dealing with conflict reflect patterns you observed while growing up?

3. Pick a situation in which someone with whom you are talking seems defensive. Consciously engage in supportive communication behaviors and avoid ones likely to produce defensiveness. Analyze what happens in terms of the other person's comfort and communication.

4. Analyze your responses to conflict in terms of the exit-voice-loyalty-neglect model discussed in the text. How often do you use each response style in your friendships and romantic relationships? Which style do you use least? What are the results of the way(s) you respond to conflict?

5. Describe a situation in which you had a conflict with a close friend or romantic partner and you managed to work it out constructively. Analyze what happened by discussing how your and your partner's behaviors followed or violated principles for effective conflict discussed in the text.

PANEL IDEA

1. Invite volunteer or paid staff members from local dispute settlement centers (also called mediation centers) to talk with your class. Ask the guests to identify common patterns that they perceive in the conflict and communication styles of individuals who are unable to resolve their differences. Also ask guests to explain their methods of reframing conflict strategies. If the guests are willing, they could conduct a mini-workshop in which students in the class participate in mediating conflicts.

DISCUSSION QUESTIONS

1. Review the concept of 'grace.' Can you recall an incident in which you could have chosen to be graceful but were not? Why weren't you? Would you do things differently, if you had the chance? Has there been a time when you

exhibited grace, although you didn't have to? Why did you choose that communication behavior?

2. E-mail a professional in the field of work you plan to enter or return to after completing college. Ask your interviewee to describe the kind of climate that is most effective in his or her work situation. Ask what specific kinds of communication foster and impede a good working climate. How do your interviewee's perceptions relate to material covered in this chapter?

INTERNET WEB PAGE RESOURCES

American Arbitration Association
> http://www.adr.org/

Anti-Defamation League
> http://www.adl.org

Berghof Research Center for Constructive Conflict Management
> http://www.berghof-center.org/

Campus Conflict Resolution Resources
> http://www.campus-adr.org/

Colorado Institute for Conflict Resolution and Creative Leadership
> http://www.weinholds.org/confcons.htm

Conflict Management Initiatives
> http://www.cmi-salem.org/indexIE.htm

Institute of Conflict Management
> http://www.conflictmanagement.org/

International Association for Conflict Management
> http://www.iacm-conflict.org/

Permanent Court of Arbitration
> http://www.pca-cpa.org/

Self-Actualization Growth Education
> http://www.sagegoals.com/

Chapter 4:
Engaging in Verbal Communication

I.   In using language we define ourselves, others, and all the phenomena in our world.

II.   Language consists of symbols that are used to represent people, events, and all that goes on around and in us.
   A. Verbal communication refers to the spoken or written word.
   B. Nonverbal communication includes symbols other words.

III.   Three qualities of language.
   A. It is arbitrary.
      1. The symbols employed are not intrinsically connected to the phenomena they represent.
      2. Meanings are fluid; they change over time as the people who use it change.
      3. New words are coined to represent new phenomena or revised perspectives on familiar phenomena.
   B. It is ambiguous.
      1. Meanings are not always precise nor are they fixed for all time.
      2. Within a culture most words have an agreed upon range of meaning.
      3. Meaning is more variable across cultures.
   C. It is abstract.
      1. It is not concrete, nor tangible.
      2. It varies in the degree of abstractness.
      3. The potential for confusion swells with increased abstractness.

IV.   Three key principles of communication in the creation of meaning.
   A. Interpretation creates meaning.
      1. Interpretation is an active, creative process used to make sense of experiences.
      2. How one interprets the symbols communicated has as much to do with you as the interpreter as with what others have communicated.
   B. Communication is guided by rules.
      1. Rules guide when and what to communicate and how to interpret another's communication.
      2. For the most part we are not conscious of the rules that guide us.
      3. Communication rules are shared understandings among members of a particular culture or social group about what communication means and what behaviors are appropriate in various situations.
      4. Regulative rules regulate interaction by specifying where, when, how, and with whom to talk about various topics.

          5. Constitutive rules define what various types of communication mean, or stands for.

    C. How we punctuate communication affects the meanings we attribute to communication.

          1. Punctuation marks a flow of activity into meaningful units.

          2. Punctuation defines where communication episodes start and stop.

          3. Punctuation is subjective, so there is no absolutely correct way to punctuate any interaction.

V.   Six symbolic abilities affect our lives profoundly.

    A. Language defines phenomena.

          1. The symbols we use affect how we think and feel.

          2. The way we name, or label, define phenomena and shape what they mean to us.

          3. A label directs our attention to certain aspects and away from others.

          4. Totalizing occurs when we respond to a person as if one label totally represents what she or he is.

    B. Language evaluates phenomena.

          1. Language is not neutral; it is laden with values.

          2. Loaded language consists of words that strongly slant perceptions.

    C. Language organizes experiences.

          1. The meanings of words vary depending upon the category into which we place the person speaking them.

          2. Organizational quality of symbols allow us to think about abstract concepts.

          3. Stereotypes involve thinking in broad generalizations about a whole class of people or phenomena.

          4. While we need to generalize to function effectively, stereotyping can blind us to the important and unique differences between phenomena we lump together in generalizations.

    D. Language allows us to think hypothetically about experiences and ideas that are not part of our concrete reality.

          1. We can think in all three dimensions of time even though we exist in the present.

          2. We can think of alternatives to what exists.

    E. Language allows us to reflect on ourselves.

          1. We are able to think about ourselves.

          2. We are able to monitor our behavior and the images we present to others.

          3. The *ME* aspect of self is the socially aware self that reflects on the *I*, which is the creative, impulsive aspect of self.

    F. Language defines relationships and interaction.

       1. Language is used to convey messages about how we perceive ourselves and others.

       2. We use language to regulate interactions.

       3. We use language to convey three dimensions of relationships-level meanings: responsiveness, liking, and power.

VI.   Four guidelines help us use verbal communication effectively, with clarity and accuracy.

   A. The most important is being person-centered.

   B. Use a level of abstraction that suits the particular communication objective and situation.

   C. Use qualifying language.

       1. Qualify generalizations so as to avoid making general statements absolute ones.

       2. Eschew static evaluations, which are assessments that suggest something is unchangeable.

       3. Adopt indexing, which suggests that our evaluations apply only to specific time and circumstances.

   D. Own your own feelings and thoughts.

       1. Use *I* -language so that you take responsibility for your thoughts and feelings whereas *You* -language projects your feelings onto another person.

       2. *I* -language provides concrete descriptions of behaviors without holding the other person responsible for how we feel.

Vocabulary Terms

Abstract

Ambiguous

Arbitrary

Communication rules

Constitutive rules

Hypothetical thought

I Language

I/Me

Indexing

Loaded Language

Nonverbal communication

Punctuation

Regulative rules

Static evaluation

Symbols

Totalizing

Verbal communication

ACTIVITY 4.1: Bias-Free Language

Purpose/Objective:
To help you understand how to utilize biased-free language and to practice rephrasing words in order to communicate in a biased-free manner.

Instructions:
Read the following passage, identify biased language, and choose bias-free replacements for those words. Replacement words should not change the overall meaning of the passage.

Original Passage:

Bob is a Vietnamese fireman who was born in California. One day, he got a call for a fire at the house of a 24 -year -old girl named Elizabeth. When Bob and his fire crew pulled up to the address they were given at the firehouse, they saw an old geezer sitting on the porch. 'Where is the fire, ' asked Bob. The old man was deaf so he did not hear Bob's question. At that moment, Bob heard a girl yell, 'Hey, the fire is over here!' He quickly drove his fire truck to the next street where he saw Elizabeth's burning house. Bob quickly turned on his fire hoses to fight the fire. He knew that he had to hurry and get the situation under control because he was the only man there (and men are always braver than women). Finally the fire was extinguished. All of mankind should be grateful for brave men like Bob.

Replacement Passage:

ACTIVITY 4.2: Adding Excitement to Your Language

Purpose/Objective:
To gain a better understanding of colorful language and to practice using language creatively.

Instructions:
Substitute each of the following phrases with similes or metaphors. Be imaginative in your attempts.

1. The sky is blue.

2. The test was difficult.

3. The child is noisy.

4. The man is good-looking.

5. Drugs are addictive.

For each of the following 'common' words, substitute with another more uncommon word or phrase (synonym) that is more concrete, animated, or intense.

Rich	Money	Said	Cheap
Building	Tall	Cold	Blue
Wrong	Hungry	Decrease	Sad
Love	Nervous	Asked	Polite
Tired	Fat	Bad	Spoiled
Ill	Angry	Poor	Good
Tax increase	A difficult child		

ACTIVITY 4.3: Language Then and Now

Purpose/Objective:
This assignment should give you insight into how meanings change over time

Instructions:
Review the discussion in the chapter regarding the principle that meanings change over time. Next, arrange to interview two individuals—one between 40 and 50 and one over 60 years old—to find out what the words below meant to them when they were twenty.

	Black	**Girl**	**Gay**	**Pot**
Person #1				
Person #2				
	Chick	**Crash**	**Rap**	**Straight**
Person #1				
Person #2				
	Bad	**Partner**	**Pig**	**Grass**
Person #1				
Person #2				
	Queer	**Ball**	**Heavy**	**Downer**
Person #1				
Person #2				

Review the answers they interviewees provide to discover what meaning these words held years ago. Be sensitive to variations in meaning that arise from interviewees' race, sex, or sexual preference, and remember that meanings are subjective.

ACTIVITY 4.4: Euphemisms

Purpose/Objective:
This activity is a quick way to heighten your awareness of the importance we attach to connotative meanings of language.

Instructions:
Below is a list of six words that are often considered 'taboo' in the culture of the United States. Identify as many euphemisms as you can that people use to avoid saying these 'taboo' words.

Euphemisms
for 'Death': _____, _____, _____, _____, _____,

_____, _____, _____, _____, _____.

Euphemisms
for 'Sex': _____, _____, _____, _____, _____,

_____, _____, _____, _____, _____.

Euphemisms
for 'Prostitute': _____, _____, _____, _____, _____,

_____, _____, _____, _____, _____.

Euphemisms
For 'Vomit': _____, _____, _____, _____, _____,

_____, _____, _____, _____, _____.

Euphemisms
for 'Fight': _____, _____, _____, _____, _____,

_____, _____, _____, _____, _____.

Euphemisms
for 'Bathroom': _____, _____, _____, _____, _____,

_____, _____, _____, _____, _____.

Can you think of other words that have a long list of euphemisms associated with them?

Euphemisms for '_____': _____, _____, _____.

Euphemisms for '_____': _____, _____, _____.

Euphemisms for '_____': _____, _____, _____.

ACTIVITY 4.5: Breaking the Language Rules

Purpose/Objective:
This activity will heighten your awareness of social prescriptions for verbal communication and illustrate the principle that communication is rule-guided.

Instructions:
Review the chapter on verbal communication and language use. Next, several rules, both constitutive and regulative, for verbal behavior and violate them intentionally. For example, you could interrupt without saying, 'excuse me,' or 'may I join the conversation?' You might address a professor with whom you normally interact very formally by her or his first name, which could violate the rule for showing respect by using titles.

After violating the rules, make note of the reactions of those with whom you were communicating. Reflect on what their expectations of you were in terms of socially constructed rules, and what the consequences were of your failure to meet those social expectations. Think about how you felt when deviating from expectations of your society.

ACTIVITY 4.6: Media Watch

Purpose/Objective:
To discover how language can be used to intentionally mislead others or obscure the truth.

Instructions:
Using the Internet, search for the websites of several Fortune 500 companies who have recently received bad publicity in the news. For example, you might look for a tire manufacturer who has been accused of causing injury to people who purchased their defective tires.

On the company's websites, seek out press releases they have issued that attempt to mitigate the bad publicity. Make note of how the company uses language in an effort to put the best face on things.

Look through magazines, or watch television for advertisements by these same companies. Again note how they use language to lessen the damage that may have been done to their public images.

JOURNAL ITEMS

1. Violate one of the rules of verbal interaction that society prescribes for your sex. Analyze what happened and how you felt when you violated the verbal communication rules for your sex.

2. Attend a religious service in a church or synagogue or temple that is attended primarily by individuals whose race differs from yours. Do not take notes or otherwise appear disrespectful while in the service, but do observe the communication of both leaders and the congregation. Afterward, analyze how communication differs in your normal church and the one you attended.

3. Describe verbal communication between you and a close friend or romantic partner of the other sex. Analyze the extent to which you and the other person follow patterns typical of women and men in general.

PANEL IDEA

1. Invite one or more relationship counselors to talk with your class. Ask the guest(s) to describe common problems in couples' verbal communication and to explain counseling methods they use to improve verbal communication between partners in romantic relationships.

DISCUSSION QUESTIONS

1. Pay attention to 'I' and 'you' language in communication depicted in feature films. What happens when 'you' statements are used rather than 'I' statements and vice versa? How do you think the characters would react in a reversed situation? How would your own interpretations of the situation change?

2. Break into groups based on gender. Each group should come up with a list of words describing the opposite gender. List these words on the board. As a class, discuss your reactions to these words. How do the words shape your interpretations? How would using different words be interpreted differently?

INTERNET WEB PAGE RESOURCES

AltaVista's Babel Fish Translation Service
    http://world.altavista.com/

American Heritage Dictionary of the English Language
    http://www.bartleby.com/61/

Dictionary of English Slang Used in the United Kingdom
    http://www.peevish.co.uk/slang/

Etymologic! The Toughest Word Game on the Web
    http://www.etymologic.com/

International Journal of the Sociology of Language
    http://www.degruyter.de/rs/384_403_DEU_h.htm

Klingon Language Institute
    http://www.kli.org/

Language Games.org
    http://www.languagegames.org/

LANGUAGE – Journal of the Linguistics Society of America
    http://www.lsadc.org/language/

Modern Language Association
    http://www.mla.org/

Office of National Drug Control Policy – Street Terms
    http://www.whitehousedrugpolicy.gov/streetterms/%5Fdefault.asp

Official Web Site for the Test of English as a Foreign Language
    http://www.toefl.org/

Slang Throughout Ireland
    http://www.irishabroad.com/Culture/Slang/

Symbols.com
    http://www.symbols.com/

Your Dictionary.com
    http://www.yourdictionary.com/

Chapter 5:
Engaging in Nonverbal Communication

I. Definition: Nonverbal communication is all aspects of communication other than words themselves.
    A. Nonverbal communication includes sounds and how words are uttered (inflection, volume).
    B. Nonverbal communication is estimated to account for 65% to 93% of the total meaning of communication.
    C. Nonverbal communication can even be more powerful than using words.

II. There are 5 principles of nonverbal communication.
    A. Nonverbal communication can be ambiguous.
       1. Meanings vary over time.
       2. Meanings vary according to context.
       3. Nonverbal communication is guided by rules
          a. Constitutive rules tell us what counts.
          b. Regulative rules tells us what is appropriate or inappropriate.
    B. Nonverbal behavior can interact with verbal communication in five ways.
       1. Nonverbal behaviors may repeat verbal messages.
       2. Nonverbal behaviors may highlight aspects of verbal messages.
       3. Nonverbal behavior may complement or add to words.
       4. Nonverbal behaviors may contradict verbal communication.
       5. Nonverbal behaviors can substitute for words.
    C. Nonverbal behavior can regulate interaction.
    D. Nonverbal behavior can be a powerful tool in establishing relationship-level meanings.
       1. Nonverbal behavior can express responsiveness.
       2. Nonverbal behaviors are keen indicators of how we feel about others.
       3. Nonverbal behavior can be a means to exert control and negotiate status.
    E. Nonverbal communication reflects cultural values.
       1. We learn nonverbal behaviors in the process of being socialized into our culture.
       2. Different cultures teach distinct values and nonverbal behaviors to express them.

III. There are nine forms of nonverbal communication.
    A. Kinesics are motions of face and body.
       1. Body posture and gestures can communicate moods.
       2. Body posture and gestures can reveal how open we are to interaction.
       3. We use facial expression to signal how we feel.

4. Our eyes are particularly important in signaling complex meanings.
B. Haptics refers to physical touch, which may express power and liking.
   1. Touching communicates power and status.
   2. Touching can reveal cultural views of gender.
C. Physical appearance is how people look and the cultural meanings attached to looks.
   1. Cultures prescribe ideals for physical forms.
   2. Physical appearance includes both physiological characteristics and the ways that we manage our physical appearance.
D. Artifacts are personal objects.
   1. Artifacts announce our identities and personalize our environment.
   2. Artifacts express gender prescriptions.
   3. Artifacts announce professional identity.
   4. Artifacts define our personal settings and territories.
E. Proxemics refers to personal space and how we use it.
   1. Space expresses status.
   2. How we arrange our space lets others know if we want interaction.
F. Environmental factors are aspects of settings that affect how we think, feel, and act.
G. Chronemics concerns how we perceive and use time to define identities and interaction.
   1. Chronemics expresses cultural attitudes toward time.
   2. Chronemics reflects our priorities.
   3. The way that we are expected to use time is influenced by social norms.
H. Paralanguage is vocal communication but without words.
   1. Paralanguage signals how others should interpret our communication.
   2. Paralanguage signals how we feel.
   3. Paralanguage affects how others perceive us.
   4. Our use of paralanguage is influenced by gender and culture.
I. Silence is the absence of communicated sound.
   1. Silence can symbolize contentment or disapproval.
   2. Silence can communicate awkwardness.
   3. As with other forms of communication, the meaning of silence is culturally linked.

IV.   There are two guidelines that are useful for improving nonverbal communication.
A. Monitor your nonverbal communication to increase the likelihood that others will perceive you and your communication in the ways you intend.
B. Be tentative when interpreting others' nonverbal communication.

1. Be aware that nonverbal behavior is ambiguous and varies among people.
2. Be aware that nonverbal communication is affected by the contextual factors.

Vocabulary Terms

Artifacts

Chronemics

Environmental factors

Haptics

Kinesics

Paralanguage

Physical appearance

Proxemics

Silence

Socialization

ACTIVITY 5.1: Violating the Nonverbal Rules

Purpose/Objective:
This exercise should make apparent the tacit, unwritten rules people have for each other regarding how they should behave, nonverbally. It will also demonstrate how different types of nonverbal communication take place in everyday interactions, and show the importance of nonverbal communication in everyday interaction.

Instructions:
Select several nonverbal 'rules' that you wish to intentionally violate in order to observe to effect. In conducting this activity, do not do anything that will cause physical or emotional harm other people or to yourself. After your 'research' is completed, the participants have the right to know they were part of an experiment and what the experiment involved.

For example, you could violate personal space by standing too close to a person in an elevator, sitting too close to a person in the library when there are open spots near by, or sitting too close to a stranger in a mostly empty movie theatre. Breach rules of territoriality in a class where people have established seating assignments by repetition by sitting in someone else's 'regular' seat. Other behaviors might include:

Entering into a conversation between a group of people you do not know. While talking to someone, make eye contact with a space six inches to the right of their eyes. Or, making sustained eye contact with a stranger in a public place, such as a restaurant, and continue to stare at this person. While talking on the phone, you violate turn taking by remaining silent after the other person has stopped speaking. During a conversation, continue to slowly move closer to your partner. Then, slowly move further away from your partner. Dress in dirty, torn clothes and go into an expensive clothing store at the mall, pretending to shop. Return a day two later dressed in your best outfit.

After concluding the activities, reflect on what kinds of social norms exist for the nonverbal behaviors you violates. How did you feel, and how do you suppose others felt when you breached those norms. What were you communicating with your nonverbal behaviors?

ACTIVITY 5.2: Alphabetizing Yourselves

Purpose/Objective:
To illustrate how some group activities can be completed without the use of verbal communication.

Instructions:
The next time you are with a group of people and wish to play a 'party game,' try this activity.

Instruct everyone that their task is to alphabetize themselves by their middle name. However, they are not allowed to use any words, spoken, written, or signed, in carrying out the task.

Depending on the number of people, it may take from 10-20 minutes. When they 'look' finished ask them to call out their middle names, beginning with the first person.

Reflect on how close they came to accurately organizing themselves. Why were they, or were they not successful? What nonverbal methods and strategies did people use to complete the activity? Were they efficient or inefficient in their nonverbal communication?

ACTIVITY 5.3: Communicating Without Words

Purpose/Objective:
This activity will clarify the importance of nonverbal communicating in expressing three dimensions of relational meaning: liking, power, and responsiveness.

Instructions:
Review the textbook's discussion of nonverbal communication and its power to express relational meanings (liking, responsiveness, and power).

Find a place in the Student Center, Dining Hall, library, or other heavily trafficked area from which you can unobtrusively observe others nonverbal behaviors.

Liking: Look for people demonstrating liking or disliking of others through their nonverbal behaviors. Look for people exhibiting specific nonverbal cues that express hostility or affection through their eye behavior, stance, facial expression, use of space, gestures, etc.

Power: Next, look for people who are communicating power through their nonverbal behaviors. Observe how the person in the superior power position nonverbally communicates his or her power over the other person(s), and how the other nonverbally expresses her or his subordinate status.

Responsiveness: Finally, look for people who are communicating interest and involvement in others through their nonverbal behaviors. Also, look for someone who demonstrates disinterest or expresses boredom through their nonverbal communication.

ACTIVITY 5.4: Inclusive/Exclusive Nonverbals

Purpose/Objective:
This activity should increase your awareness of how inclusion and exclusion to different groups is communicated nonverbally.

Instructions:
Visit campus buildings and hang-outs in an effort to notice nonverbal elements such as where buildings are located and the graffiti, books, artwork, and so forth in buildings. Also observe whether ramps and elevators exist for people with physical disabilities and whether doors have Braille nameplates so people with visual impairments can locate offices and restrooms.

Based on your observations, draw conclusions about the extent to which their campus in general and individual buildings and areas in particular invite and include diverse people.

Consider the following points: How powerful is nonverbal communication in acknowledging or erasing, inviting or discouraging, welcoming or rejecting certain groups? Do people of diverse, non-Caucasian cultures feel visible and respected in buildings adorned with massive portraits of Caucasians? Do women feel included when all of the portraits of 'important people' are of males? Does the artwork in campus buildings celebrate cultural diversity? Where are buildings located: Are minority and women's centers, formal or informal, located in the center or on the margins of the campus? How could the campus be more inclusive and acknowledging of diverse social groups through nonverbal communication?

ACTIVITY 5.5: Nonverbal Archaeology

Purpose/Objective:
This exercise will clarify how artifacts serve as nonverbal communication devices.

Instructions:
Select several catalogues that contain products for sale. For example, locate a catalogue from a mail-order clothing company and find a catalogue that sells house wares and/or home furnishings.

Closely study the artifacts on the pages. How do these personal objects define or announce the possessor's identity? In what ways would the artifacts personalize one's environment? Do the artifacts in the catalogues prescribe gender, race, and/or class? What about the expression of professional identity? Do the artifacts serve to define or inscribe one's territory?

Next, check the library for a reproduction of the Sears Roebuck mail order catalogue from the late 1800s. Study the catalogue's artifacts with an eye toward the same questions as above.

Finally, based on your analysis of artifacts, what general statement would you make about the United States culture of the late 1800s? What statement about our contemporary culture do you think future archaeologists would make 125 years from now, if they studied our current catalogues?

ACTIVITY 5.6: Media Watch—Silent Films Say it All

Purpose/Objective:
To understand the capacity to effectively communicate without words.

Instructions:
Watch a silent film from the 1920s that features a star from that era. Consider how it is that you can follow the plot without having to hear or read spoken language.

How do the actors use their bodies to convey emotions? What nonverbal aspects of the film tell you that it is a drama, or a comedy? How does the director use the camera to nonverbally supplement the actors' storytelling abilities? What does the background or scene communicate about the film's narrative? Do you think actors of the silent era had to be more effective in their use of facial and body gestures, space, and so forth than do contemporary actors? Which current actors come to mind when you think of someone who communicates effectively without words?

JOURNAL ITEMS

1. Violate a nonverbal gender prescription. If you are a woman, you might restrain yourself from smiling for 24 hours, staring defiantly at others when you talk with them, or sitting with your legs and arms spread widely. If you are a man, you might smile continuously—whenever you meet people, when you talk with them, etc. Men may also violate masculine nonverbal prescriptions by giving strong eye contact and abundant head nods and other displays of responsiveness when they converse with others. Analyze how you felt violating the nonverbal prescription for your gender and what responses you got from others.

2. Analyze the artifacts and environment of your room. What do these nonverbals communicate about who you are? How does their presence affect your feelings of comfort, identity, and security? What would be different if all of your personal artifacts disappeared?

PANEL IDEA

1. Invite a group of artists who rely on nonverbal communication to express themselves to discuss their crafts. Consider having a painter, dancer, musician and actor discuss the communication process as a creative, expressive process.

DISCUSSION QUESTIONS

1. Watch a silent film. Observe nonverbal behaviors of the characters portrayed. How are you able to make sense of what is happening without the reliance of words? Draw on concepts from the chapter on nonverbal communication.

2. Find three or four personal home pages (i.e. not web pages sponsored by organizations or companies). What types of nonverbal communication can you find on each home page? Compare and contrast the home pages.

INTERNET WEB PAGE RESOURCES

DanceWriting
http://www.dancewriting.org/index.html

Exploring Nonverbal Communication
http://nonverbal.ucsc.edu/

Faceprints Experiment Program
http://www-psych.nmsu.edu/~vic/faceprints/

Introduction to Labanotation
  http://www.rz.uni-frankfurt.de/~griesbec/LABANE.HTML

Journal of Nonverbal Behavior
  http://www.wkap.nl/prod/j/0191-5886

Laboratory of Nonverbal Semiotics
  http://www.is.tohoku.ac.jp/lab/nonver/main-e.html

Nonverbal Communication Resources: The Gateway
  http://www.lib.ohio-state.edu/gateway/bib/nonverbal.html

Nonverbal Dictionary of Gestures, Signs, & Body Language Cues
  http://members.aol.com/nonverbal2/diction1.htm

Nonverbal Learning Disorder Association
  http://www.nlda.org/

Storytelling in the Classroom—Beyond Words
  http://www.storyarts.org/classroom/retelling/beyondwords.html

Video and Audiotapes
  http://www3.usal.es/~nonverbal/videos.htm

Chapter 6:
Listening and Responding to Others

I.   Listening is at least as important as talking in the communication process.

    A. Studies indicate that we spend about half our waking time listening, which is more than other communication activity.

    B. Listening and hearing are not synonymous.

        1. Hearing is a physiological activity that occurs when sound waves hit our eardrums.

        2. People also receive messages through sight (nonverbal behaviors, lip reading, sign language).

        3. Listening is a complex process of being mindful, hearing, selecting and organizing information, interpreting communication, responding, and remembering.

II.   Listening includes six different processes.

    A. Mindfulness takes place when we focus on what is going on at the present moment.

        1. Mindfulness is an ethical commitment to attend fully to another person.

        2. Mindfulness enhances communication in two ways:

            a. Attending mindfully to others increases our understanding of how they feel and what they think about what they are saying.

            b. Mindfulness promotes more complete communication by others.

    B. Listening involves receiving communication but is not limited to hearing sounds.

        1. Many of us take hearing for granted.

        2. Other physiological factors influence how and how well we listen.

    C. We selectively attend to some communication and not other communication, and we organize what we selectively perceive.

        1. We tend to notice stimuli that are intense, loud, or unusual.

        2. We use cognitive schemata (Chapter 2) to organize our perceptions.

        3. We construct others and their communication by the schemata that we use to organize our perceptions about them.

    D. We interpret what we have selectively perceived and organized.

        1. Interpretation determines the meaning of communication.

        2. Effective interpretation depends on your ability to understand another on their own terms.

        3. Recognizing others' viewpoints even if you don't agree with them is an ethical responsibility of a good listener.

E. Effective listening also involves responding, both during the process of interaction and after another person has stopped speaking.
1. Skillful listeners give signs to show that they are involved in the interaction.
2. Responding involves nonverbal communication.
3. Responding involves giving feedback.
F. Remembering important parts of interpretations of the message is the final aspect of the listening process.
1. Remembering is not simply recalling literal messages. It is the ability to recall your interpretation of the messages.
2. We forget about two-thirds of the meanings after about 8 hours of hearing a message.
3. Selectively focusing our attention is especially important when we listen to presentations that include a lot of information.

III. There are two general kinds of obstacles to effective listening: situational obstacles and internal obstacles.
A. Situational obstacles include message overload, message complexity, and environmental distractions.
1. Message overload occurs when we receive too many messages to process all of them.
2. Message complexity exists when communication is particularly complex, complicated, or otherwise difficult to understand and follow.
3. Ambient noise is a form of environmental distraction.
B. Some obstacles to effective listening are internal to us.
1. Preoccupation with our own thoughts and concerns can impede good listening.
2. Prejudgments can get in the way of understanding what others mean.
    a. Sometimes we think that we already know what the others will say so we don't listen carefully.
    b. Mind reading occurs when we assume that we know what others feel, think or are going to say and we fit their messages to our preconceptions.
3. Lack of effort and energy can reduce listening effectiveness.
4. Failure to recognize different styles of communicating can interfere with listening.

IV. There are six forms of ineffective listening.
A. Pseudolistening is pretending to listen; we appear attentive but our minds are elsewhere.
B. Monopolizing occurs when a person hogs the conversational stage.
1. Conversational rerouting is shifting the topic to ourselves.
2. Interrupting can be introducing a new or diversionary topic through questions that challenge the speaker.

3. Not all interruptions are attempts to monopolize communication. Sometimes it can be a sign of support and/or interest.
   C. Selective listening can take place in two ways:
      1. Selectively focusing on parts of communication that support our views and that interest us or
      2. Selectively screening out parts of communication that diverge from our views or that do not interest us.
   D. Defensive listening occurs when individuals perceive personal attacks where none are intended.
      1. Defensive listening takes place when we assume that others don't like, trust, or respect us, and read other motives into whatever they say.
      2. Defensive listening may be confined to areas where we judge ourselves to be inadequate or areas in which we feel negative.
   E. Ambushing is listening for the purpose of attacking the person speaking and/or that person's ideas.
   F. Literal listening occurs when individuals attend only to the content-level of meaning in communication and overlook the relationship level of meaning

V. Effective listening is adapted to specific communication goals.
   A. Informational and critical listening is intended to gain and evaluate information. It requires paying close attention to content.
      1. The primary purpose of informational listening is to gain and understand information.
      2. The primary purpose of critical listening is to make judgments of people and ideas.
      3. There are five skills that we can use to be a better informational and critical listener.
         a. We can be mindful to carefully attend to what is being communicated no matter how complex the material.
         b. We can try to control obstacles and distractions to listening.
         c. We can ask questions so that speakers have an opportunity to clarify their messages.
         d. We can use aids to try to help us to recall the information.
         e. We can try to organize the information by regrouping the information into categories.
   B. Relational listening focuses on the relationship level of meaning, or the level of meaning that has to do with feelings and relationships between communicators.
      1. Relational communication requires mindfulness.
      2. Relational communication works best if we suspend judgment.
      3. Successful relational communication involves understanding the other's perspective.

       a. Minimal encouragers, responses that gently invite the communicator to elaborate, can help us gain insight into the other person's experiences.

       b. Paraphrasing, where we reflect our interpretations of the communication of others back to them, can help us clarify and figure out what the communicator intended.

    4. Expressing support, which does not necessarily require that we be in agreement, is important to relational communication.

C. Other listening purposes are to experience pleasure, to discriminate, and to make distinctions.

Vocabulary Terms

Ambushing

Defensive listening

Environmental distractions

Hearing

Informational and critical listening

Interpretation

Listening

Literal listening

Message complexity

Message overload

Mnemonic

Mindfulness

Minimal encouragers

Monopolizing

Paraphrasing

Pseudolistening

Relationship listening

Remembering

Responding

Selective listening

ACTIVITY 6.1: Semantic Barriers to Listening

Purpose/Objective:
This activity should help you understand the importance of listening actively and attentively, while overcoming semantic barriers.

Instructions:
Below is a list of words that people often have strong reactions to. In the space provided, please indicate your own reaction or first impression for each of those words or phrases.

Record your FIRST response; work quickly through your list. Use the following scale:

    1= Highly Unfavorable   3= Neutral   4= Favorable
    2= Unfavorable   5= Highly Favorable

_____ Animal rights

_____ College tuition

_____ Affirmative action or quotas

_____ Moral majority

_____ Gun control

_____ School prayer

_____ Liberal left

_____ Violence on TV

_____ Illegal aliens

_____ Let me introduce 'Mrs. Don Smith'

To what extent do you think your reaction to each of those phrases would affect your ability to concentrate fully and listen actively to a speaker's message? In other words, based on your varied emotional responses to these phrases, how would each tend to distract or assist you in listening actively to a presentation on each of those topics? What other words or phrases could a speaker use to replace or neutralize those phrases? List alternatives next to each phrase.

ACTIVITY 6.2: Semantic Reactions

Purpose/Objective:
This exercise allows you to examine your own semantic reactions to words, in order to clarify what informs the meaning of words, and how it is that 'meanings are in people, not words.'

Instructions:
Below is a list of words. Rank each word based on your immediate reaction. You need not know the meaning of a word in order to have a response. (You may, for example, respond to the sound or sight of the word.) This activity is designed to allow you to examine your semantic reactions, so be as aware and honest as possible.

Rating Scale:　　1= Highly Positive　　　3= Negative
　　　　　　　　2= Positive　　　　　　　4= Highly Negative

____1. Patriotism	____21. Gun	____41. House work
____2. Republican	____22. Computer	____42. Motorcycle
____3. Democrat	____23. Money	____43. Polyester
____4. Lawyer	____24. School	____44. Military
____5. Doctor	____25. Hispanic	____45. Marriage
____6. Policeman	____26. Islam	____46. Lesbian
____7. Dog	____27. Politician	____47. Science
____8. Cat	____28. Kitchen	____48. Art
____9. Shakespeare	____29. Pregnant	____49. Sports
____10. Feminist	____30.Television	____50. Cooking
____11. Homosexual	____31. Literature	____51. Gay
____12. Menstruation	____32. Teacher	____52. Spirit
____13. Castrate	____33. Jew	____53. Den
____14. Death	____34. Church	____54. Wedding
____15. Sex	____35. Religion	____55. Sanctuary
____16. Internet	____36. Bedroom	____56. Yard
____17. Breast	____37. Indian	____57. Museum
____18. Family	____38. Football	____58. Exercise
____19. Authority	____39. Theatre	____59. Vote
____20. Oyster	____40. Math	____60. Congress

Do you see any patterns, as you examine toward which words you are favorable/highly favorable and toward which words you are negatively/highly negatively predisposed? What characteristics are common among the words toward which you are neutral? What does your analysis reveal about your own listening tendencies?

ACTIVITY 6.3: Rumor Clinic

Purpose/Objective:
This activity should demonstrate the habits of ineffective listening and how they change the meaning of messages in serial communication.

Instructions:
The next time you are at a gathering of people, or you wish to play a 'party' game, find one person and read them the following story. Indicate that they should pay close attention because they cannot ask you questions, and you will not repeat the story for them.

> *Marvella had to get the courses she needed for graduation since this was her last term at school. She was a premed major and the requirements were very numerous and specific for that major, so she didn't have much room for substitutions. She had already met most college requirements, but she still needed one more historical course and one more humanities course. Otherwise, what she needed were two advanced biology courses, and both were already full, and one particle chemistry course, which she dreaded since chemistry was a particularly rough science for her. Marvella knew what she needed, but her advisor was not in his office and she didn't know how to cut through the red tape to get the classes she needed.*

After reading the story to the person, ask that they find another person to who they should repeat the story as accurately as they can. They should not answer any questions, nor should they tell the story more than once. At the conclusion of the telling, they should instruct the listener to locate another person and, as accurately as possible, tell the story.

The story should be repeated, one person at a time, until it has circulated among the group of people. Once it has completed its journey, gather people together and in reverse order, have them tell aloud what they remember of the story. You, as the last person, should read to story so everyone knows its original form and can consider how the story mutated during its retellings.

Discuss how the story changed and got distorted as it was told and retold. How could attention to listening skills have improved the retention of the story's original form?

ACTIVITY 6.4: Are You Listening To Me?

Purpose/Objective:
This activity should give you an experiential understanding of different listening and nonlistening styles and the quality of communication they foster.

Instructions:
Find a place where you can observe two or more people engaged in a conversation. Try to determine who is practicing which listening or nonlistening behaviors.

Specifically, note specific examples of any of the following:

Listening
> Mindfulness
> Responsiveness (verbal & nonverbal feedback)
> Suspension of judgment
> Taking dual perspectives
> Paraphrasing
> Expressing support

Nonlistening
> Pseudolistening
> Monopolizing
> Selective listening
> Defensive listening
> Ambushing
> Literal listening

After completing the observation, reflect on the overall quality of the conversation. Did the people seem satisfied or dissatisfied with the exchange? Did the participants show flexibility or change in their listening/nonlistening behaviors?

ACTIVITY6.5: Listening For Pleasure

Purpose/Objective:
This activity is designed to let you engage in listening that does not require the processing of verbal information, or critical thinking.

Instructions:
Select an extended piece of instrumental music in a style such as Classical, Jazz, or New Age. Be sure that the music contains no words. Locate a place where you will not be interrupted and play the music, listening through headphones. If you can, eliminate all other stimuli such as light and ambient environmental noise so that your focus on the music can be more complete.

While the music plays, push out any thoughts that might come into your head. Concentrate on bringing your attention to the music and nothing else. Seek a mental state where you feel 'at one' with the music.

Afterward, reflect on the differences you underwent when listening for pleasure instead of listening for information. What was it like to not try to follow the meaning of words? Did you feel 'liberated' by not having to form judgments or counter arguments to what you were hearing? Was it difficult to make yourself stop thinking through words?

ACTIVITY 6.6: Media Watch—Caller, Are You There?

Purpose/Objective:
This exercise allows you to practice critical listening skills and the ability to paraphrase during a controversial discussion.

Instructions:
Videotape or audiotape a listener call-in talk program from one of the television or radio stations where the host is giving his or her opinions on a controversial topic. This exercise is more effective if the host's opinion(s) differ from yours.

Call in to the host to express your own opinion. In doing so, be sure to expressing support for the host's view, although you don't agree. Practice paraphrasing and encouraging the host to elaborate on her or his own perspectives while expressing your own opinions.

After you conclude the call, review the recording you made to assess how well you did at listening and in what areas you could have improved. Review the calls made by others to the program and look for examples of listening and nonlistening behaviors. Consider how you would have handled the call(s) if you were the host.

JOURNAL ITEMS

1. Go to a place on campus where students gather and talk. Find a spot where you can unobtrusively observe and hear conversations between other students. Using the information in the textbook, record ineffective listening behaviors that you notice. Record effective listening behaviors that you notice. Analyze how the conversations you overheard were supported or impeded by listening styles and behaviors.

2. Interview a person who is in a career that you envision for yourself. Ask the professional to explain the importance of listening in her or his work. Ask the professional to identify the most common listening problems and obstacles in her or his interactions with others. In your journal summarize what your interviewee said and relate her or his observations to principles discussed in the textbook.

3. Analyze your own listening effectiveness. Using the textbook to guide you, analyze your strengths and weaknesses in terms of the text's guidelines for effective informational listening and effective relational listening. Identify two listening skills you would like to improve and describe how you plan to develop greater competence in each.

PANEL IDEA

1. Most campuses and campus communities include a number of organizations that train peer-counselors, e.g., rape crisis counseling, battered women shelters, academic counselors, etc. Ask one of the organizations to send a representative to your class to facilitate a workshop on empathic listening skills. Someone with expertise in listening and in training others to listen can give your students a powerful introduction to effective listening techniques.

DISCUSSION QUESTIONS

1. Describe a place where the environment makes it difficult to practice good listening skills. Describe another place where the environment fosters very good listening behaviors. Compare and contrast the two environments.

2. Access the website of the International Listening Association: www.listen.org. Look for different listening behaviors as described on the web site. Compare and contrast the different listening contexts, such as listening in the workplace, listening in romantic or family relationships, listening in interviews, etc.

INTERNET WEB PAGE RESOURCES

American Sign Language Poetry
        http://www.georgetown.edu/research/i2/asl/

American Speech-Language-Hearing Association
        http://www.asha.org/

American Deaf Culture
        http://www.signmedia.com/info/adc.htm

Body Language
        http://digilander.libero.it/linguaggiodelcorpo/nonverb/

Deafness Hard of Hearing About.com Guide
        http://deafness.about.com/

HandSpeak: Visual Languages (ASL)
        http://www.handspeak.com/

Listening Skills-- Canadian Association of Student Activity Advisors
        http://www.casaa-resources.net/resources/sourcebook/acquiring-leadership-skills/
        listening-skills.html

Deaf Culture Art
        http://www.deafart.org/ - 15k - Cached - Similar pages

Deaf Resource Library
        http://www.deaflibrary.org/

Deep Listening
        http://www.deeplistening.org/

ESL Cyber Listening Lab
        http://www.esl-lab.com/

International Listening Association
        http://www.listen.org/

Listening Library-- Random House
        http://www.randomhouse.com/audio/listeninglibrary/

Sound and Fury - Deaf Culture - Menu
        http://www.pbs.org/wnet/soundandfury/culture/

Chapter 7:
Adapting Communication to People and Contexts

I.   Adaptation to people and situations is a basic communication process.

     A. Effective communicators adapt their verbal and nonverbal behavior to fit different people and contexts.

     B. Effective communicators adapt their verbal and nonverbal behavior to diverse settings and people.

II.   Communication is systemic, which means it occurs within contexts that affect how it operates and what it means. There are four principles that guide a communication system.

     A. All parts of communication interact and interrelate.
        1. Each part affects all others.
        2. A change in any part changes the entire system.

     B. Communication systems are organized wholes.
        1. The parts of the communication system function together with its other parts.
        2. We cannot understand any part of a communication system if we separate it from the overall system.

     C. Communication systems are more a whole than the sum of its parts.
        1. Systems also include interaction among the parts.
        2. Systems change over time.
        3. Most living systems are relatively open which means they interact with outside factors and processes.
        4. The more open a system, the more it is influenced by its surroundings.

     D. Communication systems strive for homeostasis, a state of equilibrium or balance, but cannot sustain it.
        1. Change is continuous and inevitable.
        2. Systems try to resist change.
        3. Systems seek familiar routines and patterns.
        4. Systems inevitably experience change from within and from outside people, events, and circumstances.

III.   Communication and culture is closely linked for it is through communication that a culture is expressed, sustained, and altered.

     A. Culture is a system of ideas, values, beliefs, and customs that is communicated by one generation to the next and that sustains a particular way of life.

     B. We learn culture in the process of communicating.
        1. A culture's values, beliefs, expectations and patterns of interacting are learned both consciously and unconsciously, and over time become internalized by members within that culture.

2. Different cultures teach different ways of communicating and associate different meanings with particular communications.
C. Multiple cultures may co-exist in a single society.
   1. Geographic boundaries do not necessarily define distinct cultures.
   2. Although most societies have a prevalent or mainstream way of life, not all groups within that particular society identify equally with the dominant culture.
   3. Standpoint theory suggests that our experiences as members of particular social groups shape the way we perceive the world, ourselves, and the way that we communicate.
   4. In many ways, nonverbal communication subtly reflects the perspectives of the dominant groups within a culture.
   5. Social communities (also known as co-cultures or social groups) are groups that live within a dominant culture and also identify with another culture that co-exists in the society.

IV. Communication expresses and sustains each unique culture.
   A. Cultures and social communities within that culture, develop different forms of communication.
   B. Of the many various social communities that have been studied, gender has received particular attention.
      1. There have been gender differences noted in games we play, the manner in which we talk and listen, and how we view our relationships.
      2. Differences have also been noted in communication patterns premised on the basis of social class, race or ethnicity.
      3. However, statements about the practices of particular social groups are only generalizations and not universal truths.
   C. Communication is a source of change in cultures.
      1. Communication may propel change directly by naming things in ways that revise understandings of what they are and what they mean.
      2. Communication may instigate change indirectly by accompanying other sources of change and defining what they mean.

V. Four principles foster effective communication between members of different cultures.
   A. The single most important guideline is engaging in person-centered communication.
   B. Respect what others present as their feelings and ideas.
      1. We disconfirm others when we tell them that their feelings and thoughts aren't valid.
      2. Speaking for others when they are able to speak for themselves is usually presumptuous and inappropriate.

3. We grow when we open up ourselves to perspectives that are different from our own.

C. Resist the ethnocentric bias.

1. Ethnocentrism is the tendency to regard ourselves and our way of life as superior to other people and their way of life.
2. Cultural relativism is when we are able to recognize that cultures vary in how they think, believe, behave and value.

D. Recognize that responding to diversity is a process that includes five responses.

1. Resistance is a response that attacks the practices of one culture and/or claims the superiority of a given culture.
2. Assimilation is giving up one's own ways and adopting the ways of the dominant culture.
3. Tolerance is a response in which differences are accepted but not necessarily approved.
4. Understanding is a response that adopts cultural relativism to realize that different cultural practices arise from distinct ways of life, belief, and value.
5. Respect is a response that forgoes judgment of cultural differences and appreciates differences in their own right.
6. Participation is a response in which a person becomes multilingual; incorporating aspects of another's culture into one's own life.
   a. Being multilingual means being able to simultaneously understand and operate in a number of cultures.

Vocabulary Terms

Assimilation

Cultural relativism

Culture

Ethnocentrism

Homeostasis

Multilingual

Openness

Participation

Resistance

Respect

Social communities

Standpoint

Standpoint theory

Tolerance

Understanding

ACTIVITY 7.1: Generations

Purpose/Objective:
To gain a better understanding of age groups as a co-culture, and to practice your intercultural communication skills.

Instructions:
Intergenerational Communication Activity

Select a family member who is either about 25-30 years older, or 25-30 years younger than you are to interview. (If you don't have access to a family member you may select some other person who fits the age criteria. Retirement homes will have people willing to speak with you). Your purpose for this interview is to uncover cultural aspects of your family's, or another family's history that interest you.

Plan your interview by preparing at least 10 questions ahead of time (see the chapter on interviewing for interviewing guidelines.) Set up the interview: allow approximately 1-2 hours to complete the interview. Ask for permission to take brief notes during the interview and jot down answers.

After the interview, review your notes to discover what you've learned about this age culture, and your ability to communicate interculturally.

ACTIVITY 7.2: Role Playing Games as Systems

Purpose/Objective:
This activity will give you a concrete understanding of how systems function and of the principles that describe and explain systems.

Instructions:
Review the textbook's discussion of what systems are and how they function and then engage in a role playing game to get a clearer sense of how systems work.

Using the Internet, research 'Live Role Playing' (LRP) communities or societies such as Pagga.com [http://www.pagga.com/]. In these communities, game players assume the roles of fictional characters or build drama based on historical or living people, places, or events.

If you have difficulty locating an LRP, or the scenarios do not appeal to you, you might wish to play commercial computer-based role playing games (RPG) such as *Age of Empires Collector's Edition* (Microsoft), *Age of Mythology* (Sierra), *Civilization 3* (Electronic Arts), *SimCity 3000 Unlimited* (Electronic Arts), or *Jurassic Park: Operation Genesis* (Vivendi Universal).

As you play the game reflect on how you are involved in a system and be alert to the following principles about systems:

1. Systems are organized wholes of which any particular part cannot be understood apart from the overall system.

2. Systems entail interaction among the parts and a change in any part of a system changes the entire system.

3. Most systems are relatively open which means they interact with outside factors and processes, thus systems change over time.

4. The more open a system, the more it is influenced by its surroundings.

5. Systems strive for homeostasis, a state of equilibrium or balance, but cannot sustain it. Change is continuous and inevitable but systems try to resist change by seeking familiar routines and patterns.

ACTIVITY 7.3: Gender-Based Communication Styles

Purpose/Objective:
This exercise will increase your awareness of the differences in feminine communication styles and masculine communication styles.

Instructions:
Videotape a television program that represents a masculine communication style (e.g., news anchors, actors in a movie, politicians etc.). Videotape a second program represents a feminine style of communication. Answer the following question for each program:

1. Which style of communication does each speaker use (remember, not all men use the masculine style and not all women use the feminine style)?

2. What characteristics of this individual's speaking style led you to think this?

3. Which style of communication commands more respect from the audience?

4. Which style invites relational closeness or friendship?

5. Which style do you prefer? Why?

ACTIVITY 7.4: Naming Co-Cultures

Purpose/Objective:
This exercise will demonstrate the extent to which co-cultures exist within the United States.

Instructions:
List as many co-cultures as you can think of that exist in the United States. Start with obvious characteristics such as race, ethnicity, religion, class, age, and so forth. Push yourself to move beyond the more apparent and develop a list of co-cultures that might frequently go unrecognized by most people.

For each co-culture you list, think of two or three beliefs, values, mores, or practices that bind them together and set them apart from other co-cultures.

ACTIVITY 7.5: Responding to Diversity

Purpose/Objective:
This activity allows you to develop a set of responses to issues of cultural diversity.

Instructions:
Select a group who has undergone some controversy in their efforts to be accepted as part of a culturally diverse world. For example, you might consider the efforts waged by gay and lesbian people to have their same-sex partners legally recognized for such benefits as survivor or health insurance.

Develop a response that you would make, it terms of how you would feel, what you would say, and how you would act, as a reflection of each of the following positions:

Resistance

Assimilation

Tolerance

Understanding

Respect

Participation

ACTIVITY 7.6: Media Watch—Image Making

Purpose/Objective:
This activity will heighten your awareness of the ways in which the language used by media shape our perceptions of people and social groups.

Instructions:
Examine several newspapers and/or newspaper's websites to identify language used to represent women, men, and racial groups. Use some of the following questions to guide your analysis:

Are men and women news figures described in parallel ways? How often is marital status and appearance mentioned in stories about members of each sex? With what frequency is age stated, and for which genders? When is race noted in newspaper articles? Is race identified only when the person in the story in not Caucasian? Does this imply Caucasian is the assumed standard? Are women's and men's athletic contests given equal coverage? Are women and men athletes described in parallel ways? How much of each story on women and on men is devoted to athletic accomplishments, appearance, and personal details?

JOURNAL ITEMS

1. Interview a person (student or not) who immigrated to the United States. Focus on the individual's perceptions of differences in communication in her or his country of origin and the United States. In your journal, record what you learned about the other person's culture and your own culture from the interview.

2. Talk with one man and one woman who are at least sixty years old. Ask both to describe what men and women were like when they were twenty years old. In your journal, discuss differences between gender roles in the United States today and when your interviewees were 20.

PANEL IDEA

1. African American Teach-In. This activity should enhance non-African American students' appreciation of the richness of communication styles used by many African Americans.

   Ask four or five African Americans to lead a brief workshop in your class. The African Americans may be from your school or from the community. Explain to the guests that your goal is to make non-African American students aware of the drama, wit, and style of African American communication.

   When the guests meet with your class, they should first demonstrate African American communication practices using themselves as examples. They may demonstrate practices such as signifying, rapping, woofing, cracking (also called snapping), and calling out. [Don't worry if you don't know what these are; you can learn in the workshop too!] Then workshop leaders should get students in the class to try new communication practices.

   As an alternative, consider a panel constituted by another cultural, religious, or ethnic group that is willing to chare its own communication styles with the class.

DISCUSSION QUESTIONS

1. Visit the website of a controversial organization or group in order to gain a better sense of how they see themselves. Does their website promote feelings of resistance from 'outsiders?' Is the website a useful communication tool for fostering tolerance? Understanding? Respect? Participation? Why or why not?

2. Talk with two or three people of another ethnicity. Discuss what you learned about the similarities and differences between the individuals that you talked to. How did these interactions enlarge your perspective of each person?

INTERNET WEB PAGE RESOURCES

American Association of Retired Persons
http://www.aarp.org/

American Regionalism
http://xroads.virginia.edu/~DRBR/ayers_in.html

Black Cultural Studies Site
http://www.blackculturalstudies.org/

Critical Theory and Cultural Studies
http://eserver.org/theory/ - 5k - Cached - Similar pages

Cultural Studies Central
http://www.culturalstudies.net/ - 25k - Cached - Similar pages

Cultural Studies Resources
http://www.uiowa.edu/~commstud/resources/culturalStudies.html

Directory of Co-cultures in U.S. Society
http://directory.google.com/Top/Society/Subcultures/

Gerontological Society of America
http://www.geron.org/

Helping Children Understand Other Cultures
http://ohioline.osu.edu/hyg-fact/5000/5206.html

PopCultures.com
http://www.popcultures.com/

Popular Culture/American Culture Association
http://www2.h-net.msu.edu/~pcaaca/pop.html

Smithsonian Center for Folklife and Cultural Heritage
http://www.folklife.si.edu/

Society for Intercultural Education, Training and Research
http://www.sietar.org

Study Abroad Clearinghouse
http://www.studyabroad.com/

Subcultural Studies Project
http://www.louisville.edu/a-s/english/subcultures/

United Nations Educational, Scientific, and Cultural Organization
http://www.unesco.org/

U.S. Department of State -- Bureau of Consular Affairs
http://travel.state.gov/

Chapter 8:
Communication and Personal Identity

I.   The self is a process, a system of perspectives that is formed and sustained in communication with others and ourselves. It changes over time as we engage in new experiences.

II.   Mead contended that the self arises in communication with others.
   A. Two kinds of others whose communication influences how we see ourselves, and what we believe is possible or desirable, are particular others and generalized others.
       1. Particular others are specific people who matter to us and who affect us.
           a. In the process of interacting with particular others we gain a sense of whom we are.
           b. We import particular others' views into ourselves.
       2. The generalized other represents the views of society and the social communities to which we belong.
           a. The generalized other is communicated both by other people who have internalized the views and by the media, and then reflected back to us.
           b. Reflected appraisals come from particular others and from the generalized other.
   B. Through internal dialogues, conversations we have with ourselves, we reinforce the social values and views others have communicated to us.
   C. Self-fulfilling prophecy is acting in ways that bring about expectations or judgments of others that have been expressed to us.

III.   Communication with family members shapes our self-concepts through direct definitions, identity scripts, and attachment styles.
   A. Family members provide us with direct definitions of ourselves when they tell us who we are and when they express evaluations of our behaviors, as well as our strengths and weaknesses, or good and bad qualities (from their perspective).
   B. Families teach us identity scripts, which are guides to living and instructions on what our families stand for and who are.
       1. The process is largely an unconscious one.
       2. We learn who we are expected to be and to uphold the family traditions.
   C. The four attachment styles are basic ways of relating to significant others that we learn in our first relationship with the person who is our primary care giver.
       1. We develop a secure attachment style when we are able to trust and feel safe with others.

2. We develop a fearful attachment style when we regard others as sources of negativity and rejection.
3. We develop a dismissive attachment style, fostered by inconsistent treatment, when we view others as untrustworthy and unlovable.
4. We develop an anxious-ambivalent attachment style when we are preoccupied with relationships where we've learned that others can be both loving and hurtful.
5. The attachment styles we learn in our first primary relationship are relatively stable and enduring, but they are not absolutely fixed forever. With experiences in other relationships and with a commitment to change, we can revise initial attachment styles.

IV. Communication with peers also influences our self-concept.
   A. Communication with peers, which impact us throughout our lifetime, also includes reflected appraisals.
   B. Social comparison is the process of comparing ourselves with others on specific criteria, such as skill in music or sports, appearance, social values, and matters of race-ethnicity, economic status, sexual orientation, and gender.
   C. Our self-concepts are also affected by our self-disclosures and others' responses to them.
      1. Self-disclosure is most likely to occur when the communication climate is approving, accepting and/or supporting.
      2. Self-disclosure is revealing personal information that others are unlikely to discover in other ways.
      3. The Johari Window describes different kinds of knowledge that is related to individual growth and awareness.
         a. The open area contains information that is known both to us and to others.
         b. The blind area contains information that others know about us but that we don't know ourselves.
         c. The hidden area contains information that we know about ourselves that we choose not to share with others.
         d. The unknown area contains information that neither others nor we know.
         e. A healthy self-concept is aided by gaining knowledge in our blind or unknown areas of the Johari Window.
         f. Entering unfamiliar situations, trying new things, and experimenting can enhance knowledge of the unknown self.
         g. Information from others can reduce the blind area of self and increase self-knowledge.
      4. Self disclosure not only fosters personal growth but tends to enhance closeness

       a. Self-disclosures should take place gradually and with appropriate caution.

       b. Reciprocity of disclosure is more important in early stages of a relationship than after intimacy is established.

       c. Self-disclosure is not a primary dynamic in enduring relationships.

       d. In intimate relationships, frequency of disclosures declines over time.

V.   By interacting with the generalized other we learn which aspects of identity society considers important and how it views us as members of groups.

    A. Modern Western societies emphasize race, gender, sexual orientation and socioeconomic status, all which interact together, as central to personal identity.

       1. Race, historically privileging Caucasians, has been considered a primary aspect of personal identity in the United States.

       2. In Western cultures gender usually validating males more than females, is an important category.

       3. Sexual orientation, usually viewing heterosexuality as 'normal' is a salient identity in our culture.

       4. North American society is income conscious making socioeconomic level a fourth critical facet of identity in this culture.

          a. Socioeconomic status is not just a matter of money. It's a basic part of how we come to understand the world.

          b. Socioeconomic status influences such things as our pattern of consumption, our style of dress and appearance, the value we place on education and knowledge, our associates, careers, and our choice of recreational activities.

       5. Western society also privileges intelligence, competitiveness, individualism and ambition as well as particular body shapes and forms.

VI.   There are two important challenges to communication that foster personal growth and health well being.

    A. Reflecting critically on social perspectives is a key challenge for effective living.

       1. People tend to internalize perspectives of generalized others.

       2. Not all of a society's views are constructive nor promote a healthy society. We should reflect critically on the views of the generalized other to decide whether we want to endorse them.

       3. Social meanings are arbitrary and subject to change, and vary across cultures. This implies that the generalized other's perspective is neither universal nor permanent.

       4. Social perspectives change in response to individual and collective efforts to revise social values and meanings. This

implies that we can be part of changing views that we consider unjust, or otherwise undesirable.

B. Seeking personal growth is an ongoing challenge for each person since we are always in the process of creating and refining our selves.

1. Growth is fostered by realistic goals.
   a. Realistic goals require realistic standards (not abstract ones that are hard to implement).
   b. Realistic goals can be more reasonably achieved if they are established as a series of small attainable steps.

2. Personal growth is promoted when you assess yourself fairly and holistically, and make reasonable social comparisons.
   a. Our assessments should be measured against an achievable yardstick.
   b. Self-improvement is an ongoing process and requires an acknowledgement that change is possible.

3. We should perceive our weaknesses as well as our strengths to develop a holistic image of ourselves. It is not constructive to perceive only our weaknesses, or areas we wish to change.

4. Appropriate self-disclosure, in terms of when and how much is disclosed, can foster personal awareness.

5. Growth is encouraged when we create a context that supports the growth we desire.
   a. Context includes situations that foster the dimensions of us we wish to develop or enhance.
   b. Context also includes people who affect our self-concept and our efforts to grow in more or less helpful ways.

6. We are more likely to grow in the ways we desire if we interact with uppers, people who will give us both honest feedback and personal support for our efforts to grow personally.

7. We are less likely to achieve our goals for self-development if we surround ourselves with downers, people who communicate negatively about us and our self-disclosures, or vultures an extreme form of downers.

8. We can also communicate with ourselves and our messages influence our self-esteem.
   a. Self-sabotage is a crippling kind of self-talk.
   b. These may be repeating judgments of others or inventing negative self-fulfilling prophecies.

9. Personal growth is seldom facilitated by uncritical, positive communication.
   a. We need candid feedback on how we are doing in our quest to change.
   b. Candid feedback can be loving and supportive while still being critical.

Vocabulary Terms

Anxious/ambivalent attachment

Attachment styles

Direct definition

Dismissive attachment

Downers

Fearful attachment

Generalized other

Identity scripts

Johari Window

Reflected appraisal

Secure attachment

Self

Self-fulfilling prophecy

Self-sabotage

Particular others

Social comparison

Uppers

Vultures

ACTIVITY 8.1: Your Many Windows

Purpose/Objective:
This activity will help you apply the Johari Window to different relationships so that you can appreciate how the content of windows varies among relationships.

Instructions:
Fill out the forms on the following pages. Each is a blank Johari Window—one each for a parent, a best friend, and a past or current romantic partner.

On each form you should fill in each Johari Window by writing information about yourself that fits each pane in the window for that particular relationship. For instance, you could fill out each window with information about your dating life, drinking, family problems, childhood fears, and so forth.

After you have completed the forms, reflect on how they highlight the ways in which we present ourselves and interact differently in distinct relationships.

Relationship 1: With a parent (either parent)

	Known to Self	**Unknown to Self**
Known to Others	Open Area	Blind Area
Unknown to Others	Hidden Area	Unknown Area

Relationship 2: With your best friend

	Known to Self	Unknown to Self
Known to Others	Open Area	Blind Area
Unknown to Others	Hidden Area	Unknown Area

Relationship 3: With a current or former romantic partner

	Known to Self	Unknown to Self
Known to Others	Open Area	Blind Area
Unknown to Others	Hidden Area	Unknown Area

ACTIVITY 8.2: Changing Windows of Yourself

Purpose/Objective:
To increases your awareness of how knowledge about you that others have changes over the course of a relationship.

Instructions:
Identify a friend or romantic partner with whom you have had a long relationship. For this activity, it's important that you think about a relationship that has endured for quite a while.

Begin by recalling the early stages of this relationship. For example, think about the first 2 or 3 dates with a romantic partner or the first long talks with someone who became a close friend. Fill in Johari Window #1 with content for each pane at the early stage of the relationship.

Next, recall a mid-point in the relationship's development. It might be when you and a romantic partner first expressed love for each other or when you took a vacation with a friend. Fill in Johari Window #2 with content for each pane at the mid-point in the relationship.

Finally, think about the relationship as it is today. Fill in Johari Window #3 with content for each pane at the current stage in the relationship. After completing the different Johari Windows, review what you've written and consider how communication both reflects and generates changes in levels of intimacy in close relationships.

Johari Window #1
Time 1: Early Stage of Relationship

	Known to Self	**Unknown to Self**
Known to Others	Open Area	Blind Area
Unknown to Others	Hidden Area	Unknown Area

Johari Window #2
Time 2: Mid-point in the Relationship

	Known to Self	Unknown to Self
Known to Others	Open Area	Blind Area
Unknown to Others	Hidden Area	Unknown Area

Johari Window #3
Time 3: Current Stage of the Relationship

	Known to Self	Unknown to Self
Known to Others	Open Area	Blind Area
Unknown to Others	Hidden Area	Unknown Area

ACTIVITY 8.3: Me Versus I

Purpose/Objective:
This activity is designed to have you identify the different parts of yourself that exist.

Instructions:
Review the textbook's discussion of the self with regard to the complementary 'I' and 'Me.'

For each scenario, write our a dialogue that might take place in your head between your socially unconstrained 'I' and your conventional 'Me.'

The speed limit is 55 mph on a clear, dry, lightly trafficked highway. You are already half an hour late for an appointment and still have 30 miles to go.

'I':
'ME':

The bartender has announced 'last call' but you've already had too much to drink and are not looking forward to the long walk back to your home.

'I':
'ME':

You are not aware of anyone in your beginner's art class who has ever attempted to make a sculpture from the materials you have available—mostly an assortment of empty food containers from your refrigerator and cupboards. The art project constitutes a major portion of your course grade.

'I':
'ME':

You pass what appears to be a homeless person asking you for some money with which he can eat. No one besides the two of you are around to witness your response.

'I':
'ME':

ACTIVITY 8.4: You're Going To Be A Doctor

Purpose/Objective:
This activity will help illustrate how the identity scripts we are given when young shape our self-identity.

Instructions:
Reflect on messages you received about yourself up to the age of about seven or eight, that came from family, friends, peers, classrooms, and other social influences. These will typically be prescriptions for behaving, or direct definitions and labels of who you were or should have been. For example, you might have been told, 'Nice girls don't get their dresses dirty by playing in the mud.' Or, 'Children should be seen and not heard,' or 'you are so smart, but you don't work up to your potential.'

1. List as many of these messages as you can recall.

2. Then, note which one became internalized identity scripts that formed the basis for who you became.

3. Examine the messages to determine which identity scripts persist as part of how you see yourself.

4. Identity, which scripts you wish to change and rewrite those scripts to better describe how you wish to see yourself.

ACTIVITY 8.5: Measuring Up

Purpose/Objective:
This activity will increase your awareness of how our self-concept develops through the process of comparing ourselves with others.

Instructions:
List as many characteristics of yourself as you can think of. These should include aspects of the physical, emotional, mental, and social. Include abilities, talents, qualities, and so forth.

Next to each item, indicate one or two sources you use for comparison to evaluate yourself on this dimension and indicate how well you think you measure up.

After compiling a list of attributes and the sources you use for social comparison, review and assess what you've written. Mark each item as Healthy, Neutral, or Unhealthy. For the aspects marked Unhealthy, think of addition resources you might use to reclassify your comparison as Healthy.

Example:

My degree of compassion for others.
Sources for Comparison: Mother Theresa, Mohandas Gandhi.
Assessment: I am not doing too well in this area, but this is a HEALTHY comparison.

My body weight.
Sources for Comparison: Movie star I admire, Swimsuit Models.
Assessment: I am doing ok in this area, but I am not as thin as the people I've listed. This is an UNHEALTHY comparison and I should compare myself to the doctor's charts, which indicate that I am in good physical shape.

ACTIVITY 8.6: Media Watch

Purpose/Objective:
This activity is intended to illustrate the behaviors exhibited by Vultures and Downers, and how people sometimes engage in Self-Sabotage.

Instructions:
Videotape four or five daytime talk shows. Include a range such as 'Jerry Springer,' 'Riki Lake,' and 'Oprah Winfrey.' As an alternative, tape several episodes from different daytime soap operas.

Analyze the shows for examples of people behaving as Vultures and Downers. Note what is that they say or how they behave that typifies the label. Also look for examples of people who engage in self-sabotage. Identify what they do or say, and image what other choices they might make to avoid sabotaging themselves.

JOURNAL ITEMS

1. Read though several magazines, or watch several popular television programs, and identify examples of the generalized other's perspective. Focus on how media define desirable women and men. Analyze these messages and discuss how you respond to them.

2. Describe an instance in which you were each of the following: an upper, a downer, and a vulture. Analyze why you communicated differently in the different situations. What about the overall communication systems affected what you said and how did your communication, in turn, affect the relational systems within which it occurred?

PANEL IDEAS

1. Invite individuals, students or not, from four different cultures to discuss how individuals are viewed in their cultures. In advance, ask students to prepare questions for the panelists based on the textbook. After panelists have been introduced and had the opportunity to make opening statements, direct the discussion by asking questions such as these: Are individualism and personal independence esteemed in your culture? How important is family to individual identity in your culture? Are women and men regarded as equally individual by your culture (are women the property of families or husbands)? The panelists might also be asked to speak about what changes, if any, their cultures have undergone in recent years.

2. Invite two to four family counselors to talk with your class about families as systems. Ask the panelists to focus on the ways in which communication creates and upholds family systems and the ways in which altering communication changes family dynamics. Panelists should leave ample time for questions from students.

DISCUSSION QUESTIONS

1. Discuss magazine, film, and television portrayals of women and men (generalized other). What are current social expectations for each gender? What behaviors, behaviors, and attitudes violate social prescriptions for gender? To what extent do you agree or disagree with these social expectations?

2. Discuss any self-fulfilling prophecies you've held in the past, or observed in others you know well. What behaviors have you engaged in to promote your own personal growth?

INTERNET WEB PAGE RESOURCES

Attachment Style Questionnaire
    http://p034.psch.uic.edu/cgi-bin/crq.pl

Attachment Theory
    http://www.personalityresearch.org/attachment.html

Dissociative Identity Disorder
    http://www.nami.org/helpline/did.html

G. H. Mead—Internet Encyclopedia of Philosophy
    http://www.utm.edu/research/iep/m/mead.htm

Identity Theft
    http://www.mercantile.net/identity.html

Identity Theory
    http://www.identitytheory.com/

Mead Project
    http://spartan.ac.brocku.ca/%7Elward/

Personal Identity—Stanford Encyclopedia of Philosophy
    http://plato.stanford.edu/entries/identity-personal/

Self-Disclosure and Openness
    http://mentalhelp.net/psyhelp/chap13/chap13i.htm

Staying Alive—The Personal Identity Game
    http://www.philosophers.co.uk/games/identity.htm

Chapter 9:
Communication in Personal Relationships

I.   Personal relationships are voluntary commitments between irreplaceable individuals who are influenced by rules, relational dialectics, and surrounding contexts.
   A. Most of our relationships are social not personal.
      1. In social relationships we interact as we fill social roles rather than as individuals.
      2. The value of social relationships is in what you do rather than who you are.
   B. Unlike social relationships, personal relationships are unique and particular to the individual.
   C. Personal relationships are based on commitment.
      1. Commitment is a decision to remain with a relationship.
      2. Passion is feeling an intense desire for another person but is not the sole basis of enduring relationships.
      3. Commitment grows out of investments, which are what we put into relationships that cannot be recovered if the relationship ends.
   D. Personal relationships have rules.
      1. Constitutive rules define what various kinds of communication mean.
      2. Regulative rules specify where, when, with whom, and how to discuss various topics.
   E. Personal relationships are embedded in contexts.
      1. Both the immediate social circle and larger society are contexts that influence what happens between committed partners.
      2. Cultural values define which relationships have social and legal status.
      3. Others' responses to a relationship or a partner may affect interaction within the relationship.
   F. Personal relationships include relational dialectics that are contradictory needs or impulses that generate tension.
      1. The autonomy/connection dialectic entails desires for independence and closeness.
      2. The novelty/predictability dialectic entails desires for spontaneity and routine.
      3. The openness/closedness dialectic entails desires for openness and privacy.
      4. Dialectics can be managed in multiple ways.
         a. Neutralization is a response that involves striking a compromise in which both party's needs are met to an extent but neither is fully satisfied.

b. Separation is a response that satisfies one dialectical pole and ignores, neglects, and/or denies the contradictory pole.

c. Segmentation is a response that assigns each pole in a dialectic to specific times or spheres of activity.

d. Reframing is a complex strategic response that redefines apparently contradictory needs so they are not really oppositional.

II. While every personal relationship develops at its own pace and in distinctive ways there are common identifiable patterns.

A. A model of friendships includes six stages that may be part of relational evolution.

1. Friendship begins with role-limited interactions where we tend to rely on standard social rules and roles.

2. The second stage in friendly relations is marked by efforts to discover common ground and shared interests.

3. The third stage involves stepping beyond social roles to begin and personalize interactions.

4. Nascent friendship exists when individuals begin to think of themselves as friends or as becoming friends and when they begin to work out their own private ways of relating.

5. Stabilized friendship exists when friends are established in each other's life and is marked by continuity and trust.

6. Waning friendship involves declines in common interest or separations often brought on by career demands or perceived circumstances, and is accompanied by a degradation in communication.

B. The nucleus of intimacy is relationship culture, which is the private world of roles, understandings, meanings and patterns of interacting the partners in the association create for themselves.

C. Romantic relationships typically involve three broad phases within which there are more specific stages.

1. The escalating phase in romance includes individuals, invitational communication which marked by proximity and similarity, explorational communication, intensifying communication ('euphoria'), revising communication, and commitment.

2. Navigating is an ongoing process of communicating to sustain intimacy over time in the face of multiple changes and evolving contexts.

3. The deterioration phase of relationships can be examined within the boundaries of a five-stage model.

a. Dyadic breakdown, the first stage, involves degeneration in established patterns, understandings and routines often precipitated by gender differences in the way the relationship is viewed.

b. Intrapsychic phase involves brooding about problems and dissatisfactions with the partner.

c. Dyadic phase, which doesn't always occur, involves denying or evading problems and may include conflict.

d. Social phase involves trying to explain the breakup.

e. Grave dressing, the final stage, involves burying the relationship and accepting its demise.

4. Not all patterns of relationships evolve or devolve in similar patterns and stages. At times some stages are skipped while others may be cycled through more than once.

III. Four challenges to sustaining fulfilling personal relationships can be met with communication perspectives and skills.

A. Dealing with distance is difficult.

1. The two greatest problems reported by partners in long-distance relationships are lack of daily small talk and unrealistic expectations for time together.

2. Partners in long-distance relationships can sustain fulfilling intimacy by finding creative ways, such as the Internet or exchanging home videos, to communicate across distance.

B. Managing dual-career relationships is challenging.

1. Inequitable divisions of domestic obligations fuel much dissatisfaction and resentment.

2. In more dual-worker heterosexual partnerships, women carry most of the burden for homemaking and childcare.

3. Lesbian couples generally create more equitable relationships than heterosexual or gay couples.

4. Psychological responsibility involving remembering, planning, and organizing family responsibilities, is usually assumed by women.

C. Resisting violence and abuse in intimate relationships is a challenge for many people.

1. The abuse cuts across socioeconomic, racial or ethnic categories.

2. The majority of violence between intimates seems to be committed by men against women, and is higher with cohabiting rather than married couples.

3. Abuse is usually not restricted to an isolated incident, but instead follows a cycle from tension to explosion, to remorse to honeymooning, and back to tension again.

4. Interpersonal and cultural communication practices can serve to normalize and promote abuse.

5. Abuse seldom stops without intervention.

D. Negotiating safer sex is a critical challenge for sexual relationships in today's world.

1. Knowledge of how HIV/AIDS is spread does not translate into safer sex practices for many people.

2. Drugs and alcohol can interfere with good judgment about sexual activity.
3. Good communication skills help ease the discomfort of negotiating matters of safe sex.

Vocabulary Terms

Agape

Autonomy/connection

Commitment

Dyadic breakdown

Dyadic phase

Eros

Euphoria

Grave dressing

Intrapsychic phase

Investment

Ludus

Mania

Neutralization

Novelty/predictability

Openness/closedness

Passion

Personal relationship

Pragma

Psychological responsibility

Reframing

Relationship culture

Relationship dialectics

Rules

Segmentation

Separation

Social phase

Social relationship

Storge

ACTIVITY 9.1: Breaking the Pattern

Purpose/Objective:
This exercise should give you insight into an undesirable communication behavior you engage in with others with whom you have a close relationship. You will be able to develop strategies for breaking the undesirable pattern.

Instructions:
Think about two or three relationships that are current and important to you – a relative (mother, father, sister, uncle, etc.), a close friend (platonic relationship), a roommate, or a romantic relationship (spouse, live-in mate). Choose ones who will be in your life at least until the end of this class.

Examine the dynamics in each relationship to identify an undesired communication pattern, which you repeat with each person.

Select one of the relationships that you believe would make for a better self-study. Use selection criteria such as (1) you can interact with this person daily, if necessary, (2) this is a relationship which is of value to you and , therefore, worth your time and effort, and (3) your part in this undesirable communication pattern is one which may cause you problems elsewhere. Pick one relationship on which you will focus. REMEMBER: You are NOT pointing the finger at what THEY are doing to you, but you WILL LOOK AT how YOU contribute to this pattern of interaction that causes problems.

Write out the details of several instances when the undesirable communication behavior occurred. Try to determine when the pattern usually emerges and why it exists (remember, no blaming)?

Next, describe possible ways you could improve your interaction with this person. (Be sure to use the course concepts from your readings, as strategy possibilities.) What are possible alternatives and communication strategies you could use? (Describe several alternatives to choose from. The more specific you are about your plan, the better).

Try one of these strategies on your communication partner. Discuss what exactly happened. Why was your plan successful, OR why was your plan not successful? Identify what your ideal communication goal is for your interactions with this person. What will your communication 'look like' once you have achieved this goal? Describe clearly a specific interaction that meets (in your imagination) this goal, or met (if you had an interaction in which you actually experienced your ideal).

ACTIVITY 9.2: Supportive Communication Climates

Purpose/Objective:
This exercise provides you with concrete examples of communication that helps to create supportive and defensive interpersonal climates. The exercise also emphasizes our capacity to use communication to improve unhealthy interpersonal climates.

Instructions:
Read through the following dialogues and identify specific types of communication that contribute to the defensive climate. You should look for examples of evaluation, strategy, superiority, neutrality, control, and certainty. Consider how these forms of communication foster a negative climate.

Next, re-script each dialogue so that using supportive types of communication creates a more supportive climate.

SCENE A: A woman and her husband are driving in the late afternoon. They have been on the road for four hours and still have three hours to drive to reach their destination.

Passenger: You're driving too fast.
Driver: I'm a good driver. I know what I'm doing.
Passenger: You're going to have an accident if you keep speeding. I'm warning you.
Driver: Well, if I do it will be MY first accident!
Passenger: I may have had accidents, but you have the world record for speeding tickets.

SCENE B: A professor and student are discussing a paper which received a C- grade from the professor.

Student: I don't see why you gave me a C on my paper.
Prof: I didn't GIVE you any grade. You earned a C.
Student: But I worked very hard on this paper and I thought it showed that I understand the readings. Nothing in your comments tells me what is missing.
Prof: You ought to know what's missing without my having to spell it out for you. You will learn a lot more by figuring out for yourself why the paper is weak than by having me simply tell you.
Student: I feel you're really putting me in a double bind. You're being unhelpful and rigid.
Prof: Am I really? Well, calling me names certainly doesn't make me more like to try to help you.

ACTIVITY 9.3: Moving through Friendship

Purpose/Objective:
This activity is designed to let you see how communication varies in each stage of friendship and romantic/intimate relationships.

Instructions:
Review the stage model of friendship discussed in the textbook. Construct a brief dialogue between two people to illustrate the relationship characterized by each stage. Be sure to consider both verbal and nonverbal communication behaviors that mark each stage.

Keep in mind that friendships become more personal, disclosive, and informal as relationships grow and that distance, awkwardness in communication and less personal disclosures tend to characterize a relationships that is waning or temporarily suspended.

Repeat this exercise, substituting a romantic, intimate relationship for the friendship.

ACTIVITY 9.4: What's My Style?
THE LOVE ATTITUDES TEST *Hendricks & Hendricks* (1986)

Purpose/Objective:
This exercise will give you an opportunity to examine your own attitude toward love.

Instructions:
Review the textbook's discussion of the various attitudes toward love. Indicate next to each question how strongly you agree or disagree with the statement, then total your score to determine your primary and secondary attitude tow\ward love.

1 strongly disagree	3 neutral	4 agree
2 disagree		5 strongly agree

Part 1: Love Statements

Eros questions
_____1. My partner and I were attracted to each other immediately when we first met.
_____2. My partner and I have the right physical 'chemistry' between us.
_____3. Our lovemaking is very intense and satisfying.
_____4. I feel that my partner and I were meant for each other.
_____5. My partner and I became physically or emotionally involved rather quickly.
_____6. My partner and I really understand each other.
_____7. My partner fits my ideal standards of physical beauty/handsomeness.

Ludus questions
_____8. I try to keep my partner a little uncertain about my commitment to him/her.
_____9. I believe that what my partner doesn't know about me won't hurt him/her.
_____10. I have sometimes had to keep two of my partners from finding out about each other.
_____11. I can get over love affairs pretty easily.
_____12. My partner would get upset if she/he knew of some of the things I've done with other people.
_____13. When my partner gets too dependent on me, I want to back off a little.
_____14. I enjoy playing the 'game of love' with a number of different partners.

Storge questions
_____15. It is hard to say exactly where the friendship ends and the love begins.
_____16. I cannot love unless I've first had caring for a while.
_____17. I still have good friendships with almost everyone with whom I have ever been involved in a love relationship.
_____18. The best kind of love grows out of a long friendship.
_____19. It's hard to say exactly when my partner and I fell in love.
_____20. Love is really a deep friendship, not a mysterious, mystical emotion.
_____21. My most satisfying love relationships have developed from good relationships.

Part 2: Love Behaviors

Pragma questions

_____22. I consider what a person is going to become in life before I commit myself to him/her.

_____23. I try to plan my life carefully before choosing a partner.

_____24. It is best to love someone with a similar background.

_____25. A main consideration is choosing a partner is how she/he reflects on my family.

_____26. An important factor in choosing a partner is how she/he will be a good parent.

_____27. One consideration in choosing a partner is how she/he will reflect on my career.

_____28. Before getting very involved with anyone, I try to figure out how compatible his/her hereditary background is with mine in case we ever have children.

Mania questions

_____29. When things aren't right with my partner and me, my stomach gets upset.

_____30. When my love affairs break up, I get so depressed that I have even thought of suicide.

_____31. Sometimes I get so excited about being in love that I can't sleep.

_____32. When my partner doesn't pay attention to me, I feel sick all over.

_____33. When I am in love, I have trouble concentrating on anything else.

_____34. I cannot relax if I suspect that my partner is with someone else.

_____35. If my partner ignores me for a while, I sometimes do stupid things to get his/her attention back.

Agape questions

_____36. I try to use my own strength to help my partner through difficult times.

_____37. I would rather suffer myself than let my partner suffer.

_____38. I cannot be happy unless I place my partner's happiness before my own.

_____39. I am usually willing to sacrifice my own wishes to let my partner achieve his/hers.

_____40. Whatever I own is my partner's to use as she/he chooses.

_____41. When my partner gets angry with me, I still love him/her fully and unconditionally.

_____42. I would endure all things for the sake of my partner.

SCORING AND EVALUATION

These section scores are associated with three main love styles that are related to how you feel:

Primary Styles
1. Eros (passionate) score: _____
2. Ludus (playful) score: _____
3. Storge (friendship) score: _____

Secondary Styles
4. Pragma (practical) score: _____
5. Mania (intense) score: _____
6. Agape (selfless) score: _____

Determine your primary and secondary love styles by adding up your score. The highest set of scores indicate your primary and secondary attitude toward love. Note that this is a snapshot of your attitudes at the present because love styles may change over time.

ACTIVITY 9.5: What's Your Style?

Purpose/Objective:
This exercise is designed to have you explore what characteristics you seek in a romantic/intimate partner.

Instructions:
Read through the personal ads of the local newspaper, or dating service to get a sense of what people look for in a partner.

Construct your own personal ad, assuming that there is no space limitation. In the ad, indicate what love style you prefer from an intimate partner. Also include in the ad your preference for autonomy or connection in a partner, novelty or predictability, and openness or closedness and your own tendencies in these dialectics. Because readers of the ad might not understand these terms, be sure to phrase your ad in an understandable way.

ACTIVITY 9.6: Media Watch—The Music of Love

Purpose/Objective:
This activity makes apparent how popular culture reflects stages in the evolution of romance.

Instructions:
Write down the name of each stage in romance discussed in the textbook. Leave space beneath each stage. Next, think about songs dealing with romance that are currently popular and to identify which stage or stages each song depicts.

Write down lyrics from the songs and analyze how those lyrics describe or embody a particular stage of romance. Try to identify connections between issues, feelings, and behaviors mentioned in the songs, and the research on issues, feelings, and activities the text summarizes for each stage in romance.

JOURNAL ITEMS

1. Describe a friendship you have with a member of your sex. Analyze the extent to which it conforms conform to the gender patterns described in the text.

2. Describe a friendship you have with a member of the other sex. Analyze the extent to which it conforms to the gender patterns described in the text.

3. Review the research on rules of friendship covered in your textbook. Analyze how these rules affect, or do or do not pertain to your own friendships. Are there other rules specific to your friendships?

4. Talk with two people who are at least twenty years older than you. Ask them to describe the rules that operate in their friendships. (Note that the concept of 'friendship rules' may be unfamiliar to people who haven't studied interpersonal communication. Thus, you may need to adapt your language and ask, for instance, about how their friendships operate, what they expect, what they count as betrayal or lack of support from friends.)

5. Describe a current or past romantic relationship in terms of the stages of romance discussed in your textbook. Analyze the extent to which your relationship followed or deviated from the typical pattern identified in the text. If it did not follow the 'standard' pattern, explain why you think it did not.

6. If you are in a long-distance relationship, explain how communication in it differs from a romantic relationship in which you and your partner are geographically together.

PANEL IDEAS

1. Plan a panel of volunteers and/or trained professionals who work with victims of domestic violence. Ask panelists to explain how and why conflict sometimes crosses the line to physical violence. Also ask panelists to discuss reasons why many victims of violence don't leave a batterer. Students often don't understand that economic constraints, as well as psychological factors, can make it impossible to 'just walk out.'

2. Invite three dual-career couples to talk about their relationships and especially the ways they communicate. Ideally, couples should represent some diversity in structure (marriage versus cohabitation), sexual orientation, and race. Invite each couple to make opening statements about the ways in which being a dual-career couple affects their interaction. With this panel it is especially important to leave lots of time for students' questions since they have high personal interest in dual-career couples.

3. Invite members of several non-Western cultures to discuss romantic relationships in their cultures. Each person should be given time to make an opening statement about romance in her or his society. Then, encourage panelists to discuss the relationship between families and married couples, the gender roles prescribed for wives and husbands, social attitudes toward divorce. Ideally, at least one panelist should represent a culture in which arranged marriages are still sometimes practiced.

4. Invite four or more gay men and lesbians to talk with the class about their romantic relationships. Caution both panelists and class members that the discussion is not about sex, but about overall relationships between gays and lesbians. Remind students that sexual activities do not define gay and lesbian relationships any more than they define heterosexual relationships. The panelists will also make this point by discussing the many dimensions of their romantic relationships. This panel can be very effective in dispelling misperceptions about gay and lesbian couples.

5. Set up a panel that features individuals who are in committed long-distance romantic relationships. In advance, ask the panelists to come prepared to discuss the challenges of long-distance loving and the ways in which they use communication to meet those challenges.

DISCUSSION QUESTIONS

1. Think of three of your favorite movies. How are friendships and/or love and commitment depicted in these movies? Were the rules of friendship in evidence? Did romantic relationships follow the development patterns described in the textbook? Why or why not?

2. Think of a time when you had to negotiate intimacy (kissing, hugging, safe sex, etc.). What relationship dialectics were present? How did you and your partner negotiate the tensions?

INTERNET WEB PAGE RESOURCES

Center For Domestic Violence Prevention
    http://www.cdvp.org/

Centers for Disease Control and Prevention
    http://www.cdc.gov

Emotional Intelligence
    http://eqi.org/

EPals.com
> http://www.epals.com/

Family and Relationships
> http://helping.apa.org/family/

Friendship Page
> http://www.friendship.com.au/

International Association for Relationship Research
> http://www.iarr.org/

Journal of Social and Personal Relationships
> http://www.jspr.org/

National Library of Medicine
> http://www.nlm.nih.gov/

Relate: Information On Relationships, Family, Love And Life
> http://www.relate.gov.au/

Teen Relationships Website
> http://www.teenrelationships.org/

Chapter 10:
Communication in Groups and Teams

I.   For all types of groups, communication is a primary influence on productivity and the climate of interactions.

II.   Groups are three or more individuals who interact over time, depend on each other, and follow shared rules of conduct to reach a common goal.
      A. To be a group, people must interact.
            1. Members of a group must have a common goal even if they have individual goals that differ from the collective goal.
            2. Members perceive themselves as interdependent.
      B. A team is a special kind of group.
            1. Teams are marked by different members each who bring unique and complementary resources.
            2. More than other groups, teams have an especially strong sense of collective identity.
            3. All teams are groups, but not all groups are teams.
      C. Constitutive and regulative rules organize individuals into a unit with common understandings.
      D. Groups have shared goals or objectives. If a common goal dissolves, the group disbands or redefines its purpose.

III.   Six kinds of groups are prevalent in business and civic life.
      A. Project teams include members with expertise pertinent to different facets of a project.
      B. Focus groups are used to find out what people think about an idea, product, issue or person.
      C. Brainstorming groups are used to generate creative ideas but not to judge them.
      D. Advisory groups provide expert briefing to an individual or group that is empowered to make a decision.
      E. Quality circles include three or more individuals who mix different areas of expertise and who work together to improve quality in the organization.
      F. Decision-making groups make decisions and decide policies.

IV.   Groups have both potential strengths and weaknesses.
      A. There are two primary potential limitations of groups.
            1. Groups take more time than individuals to make decisions, generate ideas, and so forth.
            2. Groups have the potential to suppress individuals and encourage conformity.
                 a. One kind of conformity arises when a minority or single individual holds a different opinion(s) than the majority and is under pressure to abandon these and comply.

    b. A second kind of conformity arises with a charismatic member, or one who holds more power than others, and may persuade other members to comply with his/her views.

  B. There are four important potential strengths of groups in comparison to individuals.

    1. Groups have greater resources.

    2. Groups tend to be more thorough than individuals, in part because members act as a check and balance system on each other.

    3. Groups are generally more creative than individuals.

    4. Groups can generate commitment to decisions.

V. Five features of groups influence communication in groups and effectiveness of group interaction.

  A. Cohesion is the degree of closeness, or the sense of collective identity.

    1. Cohesion tends to increase members' satisfaction with groups.

    2. Cohesion tends to increase members' commitment to group decisions and ideas.

    3. Cohesion is fostered by communication that emphasizes the group and common goals and that expresses respect, affection, and inclusion for all members.

    4. Too much cohesion can result in groupthink, which exists when members of a group cease to think critically and independently.

  B. Group size affects interaction among members.

    1. Five members seem to be the ideal size for a small group.

    2. Too few members may lead to restraining criticism for fear that this could alienate and weaken the small circle.

    3. As group size increases, the contributions from each tend to decrease resulting in frustration and dissatisfaction among the members.

  C. The power structure of a group influences participation.

    1. Power is the ability to influence others.

    2. Power over is the ability to help or harm others.

    3. Power to is the ability to empower others to reach their goals.

    4. Members with higher power tend to be centers of communication; they talk more and others talk more to them than members with less power.

    5. Social climbing is the process of attempting to increase status in a group by winning the approval of members with greater power.

  D. Interaction patterns in a group affect communication and satisfaction.

    1. Centralized patterns exist when one or two group members occupy key positions so that a great deal of communication passes through them.

    2. Decentralized patterns exist when all members have roughly equal power.

   3. Decentralized patterns tend to promote more balanced communication.
 E. Groups develop norms, which are standardized guidelines how members act and interact with one another.
   1. Groups may have norms relevant to both trivial and consequential matters.
   2. Norms grow out of members' interactions with each other.

VI. There are three challenges for effective communication in groups and teams.
 A. Constructive participation includes communication that deals with the group task, that organizes group work, and that enhances group climate.
   1. Task communication focuses on the problem, issues, and information that the group needs to work with.
   2. Procedural communication helps a group get organized and to stay on track in its decision-making.
   3. Climate communication creates and maintains an environment where members are encouraged to contribute freely and to evaluate ideas critically.
   4. Egocentric, or dysfunctional, communication is used to block others or to call attention to oneself. Egocentric communication can sabotage a group and hinder its progress.
 B. Providing leadership is essential for effective group work.
   1. Leadership is a set of functions that assist groups in accomplishing tasks and maintaining a good climate.
   2. Leadership may be provided by one person or several members of a group who communicate to establish a good working climate, organize group processes, and ensure that discussion is substantive.
 C. Effective group and team communication requires constructive management of conflict.
   1. Conflict should be managed skillfully and not glossed over since it stimulates critical thought and increases understanding.
   2. Disruptive conflict exists when disagreements interfere with effective work processes and a healthy communication climate.
   3. Constructive conflict occurs when members understand that disagreements are natural and can help them achieve goals.
   4. Members should aim to make conflict constructive by being open to different ideas, to altering their opinions when the evidence warrants, and respect other members. This is more likely to occur in a climate of open and supportive communication.

Vocabulary Terms

Advisory groups

Brainstorming

Climate communication

Cohesion

Decision-making groups

Egocentric communication

Group

Groupthink

Focus groups

Norms

Power

Power over

Power to

Procedural communication

Project teams

Quality circle

Social climbing

Synergy

Task communication

Team

ACTIVITY 10.1: Useful Icebreakers #1

Purpose/Objective:
If you find yourself leading a group, these activities will provide you with a useful resource for helping people get to know each other and to increase their levels of comfort.

Instructions:
There are a variety of proven techniques for breaking the ice and allowing members of a group to learn each other's names. Here's a sampling of conventional icebreaker activities.

1. This works best with large groups: Have people sit in a circle. Ask one person to state her or his name. The second person states his or her name and that of the first person. The third person states her or his name and that of the first two people. This continues until everyone has participated.

At the outset you should assure everyone that lots of mistakes will be made and that's okay. The goal is to learn names and the repetitive process achieves that.

2. Ask people to select some item they have with them that communicates something about them. Each person then says her or his name and any other information you might request, such as department where they work, length of time with the company, etc.

They should then explain why or how the object represents him or her. After everyone has introduced themselves, you should ask several people to name as many others as they can.

ACTIVITY 10.2: Useful Icebreakers #2

Purpose/Objective:
If you find yourself leading a group, these activities will provide you with a useful resource for helping people get to know each other and to increase their levels of comfort

Instructions:
Here are more useful ways to break the ice and allow members of a group to learn each other's names. Here's a sampling of conventional icebreaker activities.

1. Other amusing ways for people to introduce themselves is to have them pick the animal that they would be if they were an animal and explain why; name their favorite food; identify the person they most admire and explain why. The content of introduction matters less than the process of getting people acquainted and at ease with one another and involved in communicating.

2. Have people sit in a circle so that they can see everyone in the room. Hand a roll of toilet paper to someone, ask them to take some and pass it on. After everyone has a strip of toilet paper, select someone to start the icebreaker. Instruct them that they are to count the number of squares in the strip of toilet paper they took off the roll. This number represents the number of items they must tell others in the group about themselves.

ACTIVITY 10.3: Character BINGO

Purpose/Objective:
To activity allows a person in a large group to get to know other members.

Instructions:
This activity works best with large-to-very-large groups of people.

Hand each person in the group a BINGO scorecard, below. Instruct them to walk around the room and find people who have the characteristics in the squares below. They should have the person sign the corresponding square. Continue the game until someone has a straight line of signatures horizontally, vertically or diagonally.

B	I	N	G	O
Has more than one email account	is/was in a sorority or fraternity	has been to Mexico	listens to the radio every morning	does not like pizza
has given a speech to a large group	dislikes dancing	is from a state west of the Mississippi	once lived in an apartment	has not eaten "fast food" in more than a year
has had an encounter with someone famous	Holds more than one college degree	plays golf	has been stopped for driving too fast	speaks a foreign language
owns no more than one television	does not have a cell phone in their family	once lived in a state that starts with the letter "I"	knows how to create a web page	never reads the newspaper
can do a "stupid human trick"	sees more than ten movies per year	likes country music	has more than one pet	has a child/children

ACTIVITY 10.4: Rephrasing Negative or Loaded Questions

Purpose/Objective:
This exercise demonstrates ways a group member can minimize adverse group/team reaction to negative or loaded questions.

Instructions:
What follows is a list of negatively worded or loaded questions. Assume for a moment that someone from your group/team asked you one or more of those questions. In the space provided, generate a response that you might use to successfully reframe the question in an effort to minimize an adverse reaction. Do this for each of the questions listed below.

A. Do you believe abortion is the murdering of helpless, unborn children?

B. How many times have you verbally or physically abused members of your family?

C. Why should the media continue to show pornography all day long?

D. Why don't you support gays and lesbians in the military?

E. Do you support non-English versions of social service exams?

F. As a proponent of Affirmative Action, why should we continue to support minority quotas?

G. As a supporter of the war, would you send your own child to fight?

H. As a self-acclaimed religious person, you should support pro-life groups—right?

ACTIVITY 10.5: Brainstorming

Purpose/Objective:
This exercise demonstrates the power that brainstorming has to generate ideas.

Instructions:
Write down as many ideas as they can think of in response to the list, below. No idea should be eliminated during the brainstorming. No matter how outrageous, impractical, or mundane, do not edit your responses. The goal is to be as creative and free from constraints as possible during this phase of idea gathering. DO NOT STOP UNTIL YOU HAVE 15 IDEAS FOR EACH ITEM.

1. Ways to use a paper clip

2. Strategies for fund-raising for a favorite charity of yours

3. Methods of encouraging safer sex practices among people.

4. The next big phenomenon in young people's toys or fashion.

ACTIVITY 10.6: Media Watch—Films Are More Than Good Acting

Purpose/Objective:
This activity should help you better understand how groups and teams are the often unrecognized source of products frequently credited to just a handful of people.

Instructions:
Review a film that is among your favorites and as you play the credits, write down the titles of the people listed, other than the actors and the director.

Conduct research through the Internet or library to determine what responsibilities are typically associated with each of those titles. Titles to focus on include:

Producer
Associate Producer
First Assistant Director
Film Editor
Production Supervisor
Art Director
Set Decorator
Location Manager
First Assistant Camera
Second Assistant Camera
Assistant Editor
Sound Editor
Dialogue Editor
Music Editor
Re-Recording Mixer
Recordist
Foley Artist
Boom Operator
Cable Puller
Gaffer
Electrician
Key Grip
Wardrobe Supervisor
Make-Up Artist
Stunt Coordinator
Special Effects
Animal Trainer
Caterer
Best Boy

JOURNAL ITEMS

1. Describe the communication of the most effective team leader with whom you have ever worked. Does/did this person perform the leadership functions discussed in the textbook? Did she or he lead solo?

2. Reflect on your in-class experience applying the standard agenda for group problem solving. Why do you think this method has remained popular for such a long time? Did you find it helpful in organizing your group's discussion?

3. Reflect on your participation in groups and teams. Describe your effectiveness in making task, procedural, and climate contributions to discussions.

4. Describe your most and least favorite group experiences. Using the material in the textbook about limitations, strengths, and features of groups, explain why you enjoyed one group and did not enjoy the other.

PANEL IDEA

1. Organize a panel of three to five individuals in different careers. Ask each panelist to explain to the class the ways in which group and team communication are part of her or his professional life. When panelists have done this, open the class to questions from students about the role and importance of skill in team communication.

2. Invite to your class one or more individuals who are experienced in facilitating personal growth groups. Ask the guest(s) to explain to your class the principles of effective communication in personal growth groups. The guest(s) may be willing to lead your class in a low-threat exercise designed to foster insight and growth.

DISCUSSION QUESTIONS

1. Imagine that the president of your school has asked that students form quality circles to evaluate and suggest improvements to all aspects of the college. What topics should each quality circle consider? How should the groups be constituted? How should they operate?

2. Think about the ways in which you contribute to small group discussions. Do you specialize in task, procedural, or climate communication? Talk about your strengths and weaknesses. How can you draw on the strengths of other group/team member strengths to offset your weaknesses?

INTERNET WEB PAGE RESOURCES

Academy of Management
> http://www.aomonline.org/

Center for Creative Leadership
> http://www.ccl.org/

Corporate Team Building
> http://www.ebl.org/

Focus Groups-- NASA
> http://nai.arc.nasa.gov/institute/focus_groups.cfm

Focus Groups—National Parks Service
> http://www.nps.gov/phso/rtcatoolbox/gatinfo_focus.htm

Group Think and Risky Shift
> http://sol.brunel.ac.uk/~jarvis/bola/communications/groupthink.html

Human Resources Web Guide: Employee Relations
> http://www.bsad.uvm.edu/hrm/ERelations/erelationshome.htm

National Youth Leadership Council
> http://www.nylc.org/

Students for an Orwellian Society
> http://www.studentsfororwell.org/

Ten Ways to Identify a Promising Person
> http://www.nsba.org/sbot/toolkit/LeadQual.html

Using Quality Circles to Master the Classroom
> http://www.upenn.edu/almanac/v43/n05/useem.html

Chapter 11:
Communication in Organizations

I.   Organizations have distinct cultures that are created and expressed in communication.

II. There are three key features of organizational communication.
     A. Organizations are structured. The very word organization means structure.
        1. Structures provide the information on what are the roles, procedures and expectations of the members.
        2. Most modern organizations rely on a hierarchical structure, which specifies chain of command.
        3. Hierarchies may be more or less rigid.
     B. Members of an organization are connected to each other via networks.
     C. Organizations are embedded in multiple contexts that affect how they work and whether they succeed or fail.

III. Organizational culture is the way of thinking, acting, and viewing work shared by members of an organization that reflects the organization's identity.
     A. As employees interact they create, sustain and possibly change the organization's culture.
     B. Vocabularies in organizations reflect and reproduce organizational cultures.
        1. Hierarchical language, used in many organizations, emphasizes status differences among members.
        2. Many organizations use masculine language that emphasizes typically masculine experiences and interests, and may suggest to women that they are unwelcome.
        3. Language in the workplace may normalize sexist practices including sexual harassment.
     C. Organizational stories reflect and reproduce organizations' identities and members' roles.
        1. Corporate stories convey the history and legends of an organization, socialize new members into the organizational culture, and foster a feeling of connection.
        2. Personal stories are ones members tell about themselves to suggest how they see themselves and how they wish others to perceive them.
        3. Collegial stories are ones that offer one person's account of other members of the organization.
     D. Rites and rituals are practices that express and reproduce an organization's culture.
        1. Rites are dramatic planned sets of activities that bring together important aspects of organizational culture into a single event.

2. Rituals are regular communication forms that are routine parts of organizational life.
    a. Personal rituals are performances in which individuals routinely engage to define themselves.
    b. Social rituals are standardized performances that affirm relationships.
    c. Task rituals are repeated activities that help members of an organization perform in their jobs.
E. Organizational cultures are represented through structural aspects of organizational life.
    1. Roles are the behaviors and responsibilities associated with particular positions.
        a. A role is not tied to any particular person.
        b. Each role is connected to other roles within the system.
    2. Rules are patterned ways of interacting.
        a. Rules may be formal or informal.
        b. Regulative rules specify who, where and with whom communication should occur. Organizational charts are one example of formalized regulative rules.
        c. Constitutive rules specify what various kinds of communication symbolize.
    3. Policies are formal statements of practices that reflect and uphold organizational culture.
    4. Communication networks link members of an organization together in formal and informal forms of interaction.
    5. Grapevine is a term to describe a free-flowing style of communication outside the formal channels of an organization and is especially active during periods of change. Research has shown that the information is surprisingly accurate.

IV. There are three important challenges for communicating in organizations.
A. In our era, effective members of organizations will adapt to diverse situations, individuals, and needs.
B. Effective communication on the job requires skill in working in groups and teams that may be short-lived.
C. Managing personal relationships (friendships and romances) in the workplace is a challenge for an increasing number of workers.

Vocabulary Terms

Collegial stories

Communication network

Corporate stories

Grapevine

Hierarchical language

Masculine language

Organization

Organizational culture

Personal stories

Policies

Rites

Rituals

Roles

Structure

ACTIVITY 11.1: Problem Solving—Dewey's Reflective Thinking
Adapted from Dewey's (1910) How We Think

Purpose/Objective:
This exercise will help you gain problem solving and critical thinking skills through a structured approach.

Instructions:
In 1910 philosopher and educator John Dewey, in his book *How We Think*, identified the steps most people follow to solve problems. Dewey's process of reflective thinking is particularly useful when applied to organizational problems needing to be solved by groups or teams.

Dewey's reflective thinking process consists of 5 steps.

1) Identify and define the problem

Consider the following questions when attempting to identify and define a problem for group/team deliberations:

  a) What is the specific problem the group is concerned about?
  b) Is the question the group is trying to answer clear?
  c) What terms, concepts, or ideas need to be defined?
  d) Who is harmed by the problem?
  e) When do the harmful effects of the problem occur?

2) Analyze the problem

During the analysis of the phase of group/team problem solving, members need to research and investigate the problem. In analyzing the problem, a group/team may wish to consider the following questions:

  a) What is the history of the problem?
  b) How serious is the problem?
  c) What are the causes of the problem?
  d) What are the effects of the problem?
  e) What are the symptoms of the problem?
  f) What methods does the group/team already have for dealing with the problem?
  g) What are the limitations of those methods?
  h) How much freedom does the group/team have in gathering information and attempting to solve the problem?
  i) What are the obstacles that keep the group/team from achieving the goal?
  j) Can the problem be divided into sub-problems for definition and analysis?

ACTIVITY 11.2: We Need Some Organization

Purpose/Objective:
This activity should raise your awareness of the pervasiveness of organizations in various spheres of life.

Instructions:
During a one week period, examine a state, local, and campus newspaper. Go through the papers and make a list of all of the organizations represented. You should look in sections such as "volunteer opportunities" and "civic meetings," along with the news, business, and social articles that often report decisions, meetings.

Classify the different kinds of organizations into groups that seem logical. For example, you might group the organizations under headings like "non-profit" "civic" "private," "federal," "personal growth," "manufacturing," "agricultural," etc.

ACTIVITY 11.3: Tell Me a Story

Purpose/Objective:

This activity should give you a better understanding of the corporate stories organizations present to the public about themselves.

Instructions:

Using the Internet, or talking to a stockbroker, find the year-end reports of several large and small for-profit, publicly held organizations. Analyze their reports for evidence of corporate storytelling aimed at instilling in readers a sense of the company's history and legends of the organization.

ACTIVITY 11.4: What's The Law?

Purpose/Objective:
This exercise will give you a clearer understanding of the laws pertaining to sexual harassment and their impact on the policies of most U.S. corporations.

Instructions:
Using the Internet, visit the government website established by the U.S. Equal Employment Opportunity Commission [http://www.eeoc.gov]. Read their literature to gain a fuller understanding of the law as it pertains to sexual harassment.

Next, visit the websites of several major corporations and find their policies on sexual harassment. Compare the policies of the organizations with the federal law, looking for similarities and differences.

ACTIVITY 11.5: Small But Good

Purpose/Objective:
This exercise should put foremost in your mind the importance of communication when thinking about the success of any organization.

Instructions:
Visit the local Small Business Association, or go to their website [www.sba.gov]. Review their "Small Business Startup Kit" and then build a business plan for a fictitious business you might wish to start.

During the process, pay particular attention to how crucial good communication skills are to ensuring the success of a company. Especially, notice the many constituents for whom you communication must be tailor. For example, banks and other investors will expect you to make clear presentations. You might need to work with distributors who should understand your needs. You might also need to establish an organizational structure with reporting lines, if the company is fairly large.

ACTIVITY 11.6: Media Watch—It's Not What You Sell, It's How You Sell

Purpose/Objective:
This activity should clearly point out to you the high physical and emotional cost to men who feel forced to comply with organizational prescriptions for gender.

Instructions:
For this assignment, locate a copy of David Mamet's Pulitzer Prize-winning play, *Glengarry Glen Ross*. Or, you can rent the filmed version. Analyze the organization portrayed by the film in terms of its hyper-masculine culture. Focus on both action and language, while considering the following themes about men:

Men should not act like women.

Men who show sensitivity or vulnerability are ridiculed as a mama's boys, wimps, or sissies.

Men must be successful. They are expected to achieve status in their lives, and to make it to the top.

Men should be aggressive. They are expected to fight and not run from battles or to lose.

Men should be sexual. They are expected to be interested in sex all the time, any time.

Men must be Self-Reliant. They are expected to be autonomous, confident, and independent.

JOURNAL ITEMS

1. Think of an organization to which you belong. It might be a church or a social group. Identify rituals and rites in that organization and explain what they mean and how they express the organization's culture.

2. Locate the manual of policies regarding staff and faculty at your school (some schools have separate manuals for each group). What policies regarding family leave exist for staff and faculty? Does the school allow flextime? Does the school give different benefits to staff and faculty? What do your findings reflect about the campus culture?

PANEL IDEA

1. Invite a group of diverse students who are not in the class to participate in a panel. Ideally, you should have students with a range of ethnic backgrounds, including one or more white, European Americans. These should be individuals who you are confident are willing to speak honestly about their perceptions of the campus and their own experiences. Ask the members of the panel to discuss the following questions:

Does our school value whites and members of ethnic and racial minorities equally? How do you know how the school feels about different racial and ethnic groups? What activities (rituals, rites) at this school make you feel like an insider--as if you belong? Which activities (rituals, rites, etc.) at this school make you feel like an outsider—as if you don't belong here, or aren't fully valued?

With panelists, probe differences in perceptions of the campus and its attitude toward diverse ethnic groups. Relate their varying perceptions to standpoint theory.

DISCUSSION QUESTIONS

1. Think of this class as an organization. Describe some common rites and rituals. What do these rites and rituals communicate about this class?

2. Choose three organizational homepages (e.g., www.aol.com; www.disney.com; www.amnesty.org; www.toastmasters.org; www.syr.edu). Describe the organization's vocabulary stories, rites and rituals, and structures. What does each of these tell you about the organization's culture?

INTERNET WEB PAGE RESOURCES

European Foundation for the Improvement of Living and Working Conditions
    http://www.eurofound.ie/

FreeQuality: A free resource for the quality-minded professional
    http://www.freequality.org/

Global Development Research Center
    http://www.gdrc.org/

Government Online Learning Center
    http://www.golearn.gov/

Human Resources Web Guide: Organizational Culture
    http://www.bsad.uvm.edu/hrm/orgculture/orgculturehome.htm

Management Assistance Program for Nonprofits
    http://www.mapfornonprofits.org/

National Learning Communities Project
    http://learningcommons.evergreen.edu/

National Service-Learning Clearinghouse
    http://www.servicelearning.org/

Non-governmental Organizations Global Network
    http://www.ngo.org/

Organizational Culture: A Web Walk
    http://www.oise.utoronto.ca/~vsvede/culture.htm

Rites and Rituals with a Greco-Roman Orientation
    http://www.cs.utk.edu/~mclennan/OM/rites.html

Small Business Administration
    http://www.sba.gov/

Social Science Research Network
    http://www.ssrn.com/

Rainforest Action Network
    http://www.ran.org/

Chapter 12:
Public Communication

I.   Public speaking may be thought of as enlarged conversation.
   A. Many of the skills that are effective in one-to-one and group interactions are also effective in public speaking situations.
   B. In general, good public speaking is not highly formal or stiff.
   C. A conversational speaking style is appropriate in many public situations.

II.   There are three overlapping purposes for public communication.
   A. Presentations to entertain aim to engage, amuse, or please listeners.
      1. Presentations to entertain include more than humorous addresses. Included are all presentations that amuse, interest, and/or entertain listeners.
      2. Narrative speaking (storytelling) is a form of presentation that may entertain without being humorous.
   B. Presentations to inform are intended to increase listeners' understanding, awareness, or knowledge of some topic.
      1. Presentations to inform may include persuasive aspects.
      2. Presentations to inform should be designed with attention to what listeners already know and believe.
   C. Presentations to persuade aims to change attitudes, beliefs, or behaviors, or serve as motivation for some purpose.

III. Public speaking has two distinct features that differentiate it from casual interaction.
   A. Public speaking requires more planning and preparation than casual conversations.
      1. Effective public speakers conduct research.
      2. Effective public speakers practice their delivery.
   B. Public speaking involves less overt interaction between communicators.
      1. Speakers tend to dominate the 'air waves.'
      2. Listeners, however, are actively engaged and continuously communicate to speakers, primarily using nonverbal communication.

IV.   There are three steps in planning and presenting effective public communication.
   A. Speakers should earn credibility.
      1. Initial credibility is the expertise, dynamism, and character that listeners attribute to speakers before speakers begin their presentations.

    2. Derived credibility is the expertise, dynamism, and character that listeners attribute to speakers as a result of how speakers communicate in a presentation.

    3. Terminal credibility is a cumulative combination of initial and derived credibility.

B. A well-crafted speech involves careful planning.

    1. Speakers should choose topics that matter to them, that are appropriate for the speaking situation, that are sensitive to listeners' interests, knowledge and backgrounds, and that are limited in scope.

    2. Speakers should define their general purpose (entertain, persuade, inform) and their specific purpose (specification of what the presentation should achieve).

    3. Speakers should develop a clear, concise thesis statement that states the main idea of the presentation.

        a. Speakers have an ethical requirement to check the accuracy of the material and credibility of the sources they use.

        b. A halo effect is relying on a person with a reputation in one area to be used as an expert in some other area.

C. Effective presentations require research to discover evidence to support ideas. Forms of evidence are examples, comparisons (analogies), statistics, quotations (testimony), and visual aids.

D. Speakers should organize presentations carefully.

    1. The introduction to a presentation should gain listeners' attention, state what the presentation is about, and preview how the speaker will develop the topic.

    2. The body of the presentation develops the thesis by organizing content into distinct, yet related points.

    3. The conclusion should summarize the main ideas of a presentation and leave listeners with a memorable final idea.

    4. Transitions are words, phrases, and sentences that connect parts of a presentation and points within each part.

E. Speakers should develop effective styles of delivering presentations.

    1. Effective oral style is more personal, active, and immediate than effective written style.

    2. Four styles of delivery are generally recognized.

        a. Impromptu presentations involve little or no preparation.

        b. Extemporaneous presentations, probably the most common kind, involve substantial preparation and practice, but use notes rather than memorization for the delivery.

        c. Manuscript delivery involves giving the presentation directly from a completely written manuscript.

        d. Memorized delivery involves committing the entire presentation to memory and is delivered without notes.

    3. Regardless of the style, the selection of verbal and nonverbal symbolizes are important.

V.   There are three common challenges to effective public communication.
   A. Communication apprehension is anxiety associated with real or anticipated communication encounters.
      1. Most people experience a degree of anxiety about communicating in some situations.
      2. Some anxiety can improve communication because it makes us more alert and dynamic.
      3. When anxiety is sufficient to hinder the ability to interact with others, communication apprehension exists.
      4. There are different causes of communication apprehension.
         a. Situational anxiety is limited to specific situations that causes apprehension and includes such things as interacting with unfamiliar people, being in novel situations, being in the spotlight, being evaluated, and past failure in a speaking situation.
         b. Chronic causes of communication anxiety exist when we are anxious in most or all situations where we are expected to speak. It appears to be learned.
   B. There are methods for reducing communication apprehension.
      1. Systematic desensitization combines techniques for physical relaxation with thought about progressively more challenging communication experiences.
      2. Cognitive restructuring aims to revise how individuals think about communication by teaching them to identify and challenge self-defeating beliefs.
      3. Positive visualization guides apprehensive speakers through imagined speaking experiences that are positive so that individuals form a positive image of themselves as communicators.
      4. Skills training teaches skills for effectiveness in specific kinds of communication situations.
   C. Effective public speaking requires analyzing and adapting to an audience.
      1. Speakers should adapt presentations to listeners' interests, knowledge of a topic, educational levels, values, and so forth.
      2. Observations, conversations, and surveys are means of gathering information that can inform listeners of analysis.
   D. Listening critically to speakers is a final challenge in public communication.
      1. Critical listening involves assessing whether a speaker is ethical and informed and whether a presentation is soundly reasoned and supported.
      2. Critical listening begins with focusing on a speaker's ideas and suspending one's own.

Vocabulary Terms

Cause-effect

Cognitive restructuring

Communication apprehension

Comparative patterns

Comparisons (Analogies)

Credibility

Derived credibility

Evidence

Examples

Extemporaneous delivery

Halo effect

Impromptu delivery

Initial credibility

Manuscript delivery

Memorized delivery

Motivated sequence pattern

Narrative speaking

Oral Style

Persuasive speech

Positive visualization

Problem-solving pattern

Quotations

Skills training

Spatial patterns

Specific purpose

Speech to entertain

Speech to inform

Speech to persuade

Star structure

Statistics

Systematic desensitization

Temporal patterns

Terminal credibility

Thesis statement

Topical patterns

Transitions

Visual aids

Wave patterns

ACTIVITY 12.1: Ladies & Gentlemen, I am Honored to Present...

Purpose/Objective:
This activity will help you gain experience in writing brief speeches of introduction.

Instructions:
Select a famous person whom you have always admired for particular qualities that they possess. The person does not have to be alive, and can be real or fictitious.

Your task is to prepare a 3-minute speech of introduction for the person, who has been invited as an after dinner speaker for your group. Use the library and the Internet to thoroughly research the person's background and from the data you gather, write out the text you would use.

Your speech of introduction can be humorous, it could contain anecdotes that are revealing of some aspect of the person, or it could be a brief biographical sketch. Remember, your job is to shine the spotlight on the guest, not steal the stage.

ACTIVITY 12.2: Organizing our Thoughts

Purpose/Objective:
This activity is designed to help you practice organizing your thoughts in a logical manner, and to develop your skills in the art of persuasion.

Instructions:
Review the textbook's discussion of the Motivated Sequence Pattern for organizing speeches.

Write three, 5-minute persuasive speeches, each of which should contain an 30-second introduction, a 4-minute body consisting of three points, and a 30-second conclusion. The Specific Purpose of the speech is to convince the audience that Xs are better than Ys and as a result, they should ....

Speech Topic 1: HORSES ARE BETTER THAN PIGS (or PIGS ARE BETTER THAN HORSES)

Speech Topic 2: APPLES ARE BETTER THAN ORANGES (or ORANGES ARE BETTER THAN APPLES)

Speech Topic 3: DOGS ARE BETTER THAN CATS (or CATS ARE BETTER THAN DOGS)

Your group is to write and deliver a 5-minute speech in which you attempt to persuade the audience of the above claim, and to accept the policy you develop. In your speech, provide an introduction, a body with three main points, and a conclusion. Your speech should follow this structure:

I. INTRODUCTION

    A. Attention

II. BODY

    A. Need
    B. Satisfaction
    C. Visualization

II. CONCLUSION

    A. Action

ACTIVITY 12.3: Brainstorming: Introductions and Conclusions

Purpose/Objective:
This exercise will sharpen your skills in developing alternative openings and closing for speeches.

Instructions:
Select two or three of the speech topics, listed below. Or develop your own topics.

For each topic brainstorm 4 appropriate attention-getters and conclusions for each of the topics. The introductions should differ in their approach to gaining attention and in how they preview the topic. Likewise, each conclusion should bring closure in a different way.

Sample Topics

Animal Rights
Arctic Exploration/Development
Capital Punishment
Children's Rights
Cloning
Common Currency
Death/Euthanasia
Deforestation
Dream Interpretation
Dress Codes
Endangered Species
Freedom of Speech
Genetic Engineering
Green Movement
Human Rights Gambling
Life Support
Natural Disasters

Nuclear Accidents
Overgrazing on Lands
Pesticides
Pollution
Single Sex Schools
Space Exploration
Steroid Use
Surrogate Motherhood
Terrorism
Test Tube Children
The Elderly
Third World Problems
Toxic Waste
United Nations
Voting
Wars
Wealth/Poverty

ACTIVITY 12.4 : Organizing a Presentation

Purpose/Objective:
This activity is designed to increase your understanding of the importance of organization in a speech.

Instructions:
Assume you are preparing an interpersonal research paper on the **IDEAL WOMAN** or **MAN**. Your task is to generate a brief outline—including a specific purpose statement, thesis statement, and three main points and sub-points. Be sure to identify the types of organizational pattern you would use for this presentation topic. Refer to the textbook's discussion of organizational patterns to refresh yourself.

No research is needed for this assignment; just "make up" facts if you need to.

Title:
Specific Purpose:
Thesis Statement:
Introduction:
      Attention getter:
      Preview:

Body:
      I. Main point 1.
          A. Sub-point 1.
          B. Sub-point 2.

      II.

          A.
          B.

      III.

          A.
          B.

Conclusion:
      Summary:
      Memorable Statement:

ACTIVITY 12.5: Vary Your Vocalics

Purpose/Objective:
This exercise should help you gain a better understanding of the ways in which individuals express emotion through tone of voice and imbue words with different meanings.

Instructions:
Find a place where you will not be disturbed and you will not feel self-conscious speaking out. Turn on a tape recorder and recite aloud the following line:

"A frog jumped out of the water."

Use your vocalics to express one of the emotions listed below. Select another emotion and repeat the same line, again using vocalics to express another one of the emotions. Repeat this exercise until all emotions are expressed.

Replay the tape recording of yourself and assess how well you did. Recite the line again for any expressions of emotion that you think were unclear, or could be improved upon.

Anger	Reverence
Disgust	Relief
Love	Uncertainty
Hate	Surprise
Jealousy	Joy
Boredom	Pain
Passion	Guilt

ACTIVITY 12.6: Media Watch—How Was Your Speech?

Purpose/Objective:
This exercise will improve your understanding of what makes a good speech based on standard evaluation criteria.

Instructions:
Analyze the speech of a public figure, such as the President of the United States. Or, select a famous speech for which a visual record exists, such as M. L. King's "I Have a Dream" speech. Videotapes of such speeches are usually available through the library.

Watch the speech several times and then evaluate its quality based on the following criteria:

Introduction/Conclusion
Did the speaker deliver an effective and appropriate introduction and conclusion? Cite specifics of what they did right and wrong.

Audience Adaptation
Did the speaker adapt the subject matter to the audience in such a way as to facilitate reception of the information? If so, how? If not, how could this have been done this better?

Organization
Was there a clear, effective organizational pattern to the speech? Did the speaker place their points in a strategic order and did use signposts and transitional phrases? If not, how could they have improved?

Supporting Material
Was there high quality supporting material and was it used effectively? Was the material properly cited in your speech? If used, were visual aids used effectively?

Delivery Basics
Did the speaker exhibit consistent and effective eye contact? Were gestures effective and free of distraction? Were vocal techniques effective and free of distraction? Overall, did the speaker project an effective, natural communicative personality?

JOURNAL ITEMS

1. Take one chapter in your textbook and determine the organizational pattern employed. Why do you think the author chose this pattern? What other ways of organizing the chapter material might have been effective?

2. Select a teacher or other public communicator whom you consider particularly effective in public presentations. Listen to this person when he or she is speaking and note whether he or she uses the characteristics of oral style discussed in the textbook.

3. Think about a speech that you found particularly effective. Describe and evaluate the speaker and the speech in terms of organization, credibility, use of evidence, delivery, the introduction and the conclusion.

4. Describe the evidence the author of your textbook uses to support claims and advice on communication. Evaluate the adequacy and effectiveness of the evidence used.

5. Analyze your scores on the Communication Apprehension Instrument presented in the textbook. Do your scores on the instrument reflect your self-perceptions of your comfort speaking in various situations? How might you increase your comfort in communication situations that currently produce an undesirable amount of anxiety for you?

PANEL IDEA

1. Invite three or four individuals who are in different professions to speak with your class. To prepare the panelists, tell them your goal is to make students aware of the importance of public communication in professional life. Ask panelists to come prepared with examples of short and long, formal and informal, impromptu and memorized speeches that they have given as part of their professional life. Allow the panelists a set number of minutes each to speak; then invite students to ask questions.

DISCUSSION QUESTIONS

1. Find your daily horoscope in the newspaper. Read the horoscope and develop a one-minute impromptu speech that relates the statement to something in your own life. Explain how the horoscope is applicable or not applicable to you. Creativity and humor may be utilized to create a memorable and interesting speech.

2. Think about presentations that you see on TV. How much do these speakers seem to take the audience into consideration in what they say? Does this affect the speakers' effectiveness?

INTERNET WEB PAGE RESOURCES

Advanced Public Speaking Institute
    http://www.public-speaking.org/

Audience Analysis
    http://www.wsu.edu/~amerstu/pop/audience.html

Effective Presentations-- Kansas University Medical Center
    http://www.kumc.edu/SAH/OTEd/jradel/effective.html

Gallup Organization
    www.gallup.com/

Great American Speeches-- PBS
    http://www.pbs.org/greatspeeches/timeline/index.html

Microsoft PowerPoint Home Page
    http://www.microsoft.com/office/powerpoint/

Presentations.com
    http://www.presentations.com/

Presenter's University
    http://www.presentersuniversity.com/

Public Speaking Tips
    http://www.uncommon-knowledge.co.uk/public_speaking_tips.htm

SpeechTips.com
    http://www.speechtips.com/

Speech Topics
    http://www.speech-writers.com/persuasiveinformativespeeches.htm

Ten Audience Analysis Exercises
    http://www.tengrrl.com/tens/013.shtml

Toastmasters International
    http://www.toastmasters.org/

Chapter 13:
Mass Communication

I.   Mass communication is all media that address mass audiences.
    A. Mass communication includes books, films, television, radio, newspapers, magazines, and other forms of visual and print communication.
    B. Mass communication includes computer technologies through which communication reaches a great many people.
    C. Mass communication does not include one-on-one computer-mediated communication (e.g., e-mail exchanges between friends.)

II. Marshall McLuhan: Distinct media have emerged and dominated different eras in Western society.
    A. The tribal epoch was dominated by oral communication.
        1. Stories and rituals passed cultural traditions and history from generation to generation.
        2. Hearing was the dominant sense.
        3. Fostered cohesive communities.
    B. The literate epoch emerged with the invention of the phonetic alphabet.
        1. Written communication allowed individuals to gain information privately without the need for face-to-face interaction.
        2. Sight was the dominant sense.
        3. Sequential ordering of written words cultivated linear thinking.
    C. The print epoch was ushered in by the invention of the printing press.
        1. The printing press made written communication available to the masses and helped usher in more widespread literacy.
        2. Sight was the dominant sense.
        3. Cultivated greater homogeneity as more people had access to the same messages.
    D. The electronic epoch was launched by the telegraph, which was followed by more sophisticated means of electronic communication (television, computer).
        1. Electronic communication makes it possible for people to know and see and hear about events and people in distant places. It moves the world toward a 'global village.'
        2. Revived the aural tradition and made hearing and touch the dominant senses.

III. There are four distinct views of how mass communication function and affect us.
    A. Uses and gratification theory claims that people attend to media to gratify themselves.
        1. In a quest for satisfying some specified need, we select media we believe will offer that gratification.

2. Uses and gratification theory assumes people are active agents who make deliberate choices to gratify themselves.

B. Agenda setting theorists argue that media set our agenda by spotlighting some events, issues, people, and perspectives while downplaying others.

1. The core idea is that the media do not tell us what to think, but helps frame what we should think about.

2. Gatekeepers are people and groups that decide which messages pass through the gates of information control to reach people. The information that gets through the gatekeepers is what we know or understand about many issues, events, and people.

3. Mass media have many gatekeepers among them owners, producers, editors, publishers, advertisers, political groups, etc.

4. Research on agenda setting has identified racial and ethnic biases in contemporary mass media.

C. Cultivation theory claims that television cultivates (or promotes) a worldview that is inaccurate but that viewers assume reflects real life.

1. Cultivation is a cumulative process that over time comes to foster our view of reality.

2. The premise is that the more one attends to television (heavy viewers) the more distorted perspective of reality they hold, a 'television view' of the world.

3. The amount of violence on television is much greater than the amount of violence that most people encounter in their own lives, yet many people think that they are likely to be the victim of violence because of what they have seen on television.

4. Two mechanisms help explain the cultivation process.

   a. Mainstreaming is television's tendency to stabilize and homogenize views within a society in order to create a single allegedly mainstream view.

   b. Resonance is the extent to which media representations are congruent with personal experiences. The more consistency there is between television reality and personal experiences, the more credible we find television.

D. Critical communication scholars argue that mass communication supports prevailing power inequities and privileged classes.

1. Some critical media scholars believe that the media detracts from democracy because only those who have a lot of money and power benefit from the media.

2. Mass media tend to represent the ideology of privileged groups as normal, right, and natural.

3. Some critical media scholars argue that mass media reinforce existing inequities between social groups and co-cultures.

IV. Two critical challenges confront consumers of mass communication.

A. First challenge is to develop media literacy similar to way we become literate in reading or with using new technologies.

1. Assess media influence realistically because the link between media and society is more complex than a simple linear relationship.
2. Learn to recognize patterns that media employ.
3. Rather than simply assimilating media messages uncritically, actively interrogate them.
4. Expose yourself to a range of media sources.

B. Second challenge is to actively respond which helps recognize partial truths and distorted worldviews
   1. Active agency is empowering.
   2. People have an ethical responsibility to resist and redefine messages that we consider harmful or inaccurate.

Vocabulary Terms

Agenda setting

Cultivation

Cultivation theory

Electronic epoch

Gatekeeper

Literate epoch

Mainstreaming

Mass Communication

Mean world syndrome

Media literacy

Print epoch

Puffery

Resonance

Tribal epoch

Uses and gratification

ACTIVITY 13.1: Image Making the World Over

Purpose/Objective:
This exercise will sharpen your awareness of ways in which the language used in newspapers shapes perceptions of social groups.

Instructions:
Read three different English-language newspapers from different parts of the world, for each of the next several days. Do not use local or regional newspapers. International newspapers may be available from the library, or you can read online version through the Internet. Try to select papers from culturally diverse parts of the world. For example, you might read the following:

The Buenos Aires [Argentina] Herald
   [http://www.buenosairesherald.com/]

The [Hong Kong] Asia Times
   [http://www.atimes.com/]

The [Johannesburg, South Africa] Mail & Guardian
   [http://www.mg.co.za/]

The [London] Times
   [http://www.timesonline.co.uk/]

Analyze the coverage for bias. For example, be vigilant for language that represents men and women in specific ways, that addresses different racial groups, religions, or ethnicities, that makes distinctions based on socioeconomic classes of people, or among lesbian and gay people. Also notice absences in what is presented in the papers.

What conclusion can you make about the media's ability to use language and images to shape our perceptions of others?

ACTIVITY 13.2: Friendly Persuasion

Purpose/Objective:
This exercise will increase your understanding of ethical forms of persuasion.

Instructions:
Prepare the text for two television or radio commercials designed to sell a service or product.

One commercial should demonstrate ethical communication practices and one should violate ethical standards.

Each commercial should be from 30 seconds to 60 seconds in length.

A) Begin each commercial with a catchy opening question or phrase that will develop listener curiosity.

B) Provide 2-3 main points in the body of the commercial.

C) End with a closing phrase that sums up your commercial.

Remember that being an ethical persuader means:

your goals are ethically sound.
you are honest in what you say.
you avoid name-calling.
you give credit to others, when due.
you fully disclose information.

ACTIVITY 13.3: Where's the Support?

Purpose/Objective:
This exercise should increase your critical evaluation of support (or lack thereof) for public communication intended to persuade an audience.

Instructions:
Select one or two examples from each of the following sources of persuasive, public communication:

Advertising in popular magazines
Television commercials
Editorials in newspapers
Talk radio shows

Keep a written record of claims made in the communication and the evidence used to support claims. Write up an evaluation of the supporting material used in these persuasive claims and calls to action (e.g., they want you to buy their product).

What conclusions can your draw about the importance of developing critical attitudes toward evidence (or lack thereof) in public persuasive messages?

ACTIVITY 13.4: World Radio

Purpose/Objective:
This activity will help you better understand how radio broadcasting media in various parts of the world differ in their approach and objectives.

Instructions:
Select four or five radio stations to listen to from differing parts of the world. International radio stations broadcasting over the Internet can be located using web sites such as:

BRS Media [http://www.web-radio.fm/in_list.cfm]

Radio-Locator [http://www.radio-locator.com/]

As you listen, it would be helpful if the broadcast were in a language you understand. If it is, analyze the content of the broadcast in terms of whether it is news, music, talk, how many commercials, if any are included, and so forth. Try to characterize the nature of the radio station and what its "mission" might be. Compare several radio stations from different parts of the world to see what conclusions you can draw.

If the stations you listen to are not in languages you understand, try to feel the rhythm of the broadcast. Does the tone of the talk seem argumentative? Soothing? Informative? If there is music, is it U.S.-centric, or does it seem modern but ethnic? Does it sound like traditional folk music? What conclusions can you arrive at about radio broadcasts from other countries, based on your listening to the "tone"?

Do you see any evidence of cultural imperialism—that is, does the Eurocentric culture or the culture of the United States seem to have influenced the radio broadcasts of other countries?

ACTIVITY 13.5: Back in the Good Old Days

Purpose/Objective:
This exercise will allow you to examine how television's constructions of the "ideal" family have changed over time.

Instructions:
Select a couple of television programs from the 1950s, 1960s, 1970s, 1980, 1990s, and 2000s that center around a family. Watch an episode or two of each program and note the demographics (age, gender, etc.) of each member of the household. Also analyze the members' characteristics, attitudes, aptitudes, and so forth. Finally, focus on their relationships with other members of the household.

What general statements can you make about how families have been "constructed" by television over the last fifty years? What similarities and differences exist between generations? How accurate do you think these portrayals have been, historically? Were there eras in which the portrayals were more or less accurate? What effect do you think these media constructions might have on viewers?

ACTIVITY 13.6: Media Watch—Bodies On Prime Time

Purpose/Objective:
This activity should point out how television creates an unhealthy "ideal" body image.

Instructions:
For one week, watch network television during "Prime Time." Using the tracking form, below, indicate the physical characteristics of every woman who is represented on the screen, both in the programs and in the commercials. At the end of the week, review your tracking form and develop a statement that describes the "ideal" women, as imagined by network broadcasters.

Age						
0-12	13-19	20-29	30-39	39-49	49-59	over 59

Weight				
Under 100 lbs.	100-120	120-135	135-175	over 175

Hair Color					
Blonde	Brunette	Black	Red	Brown	Other

Eye Color				
Blue	Brown	Green	Hazel	Other

Race			
Caucasian	African-American	Asian-Pacific/Islander	Latina
American Indian/Alaskan Native	Multiracial	Other	

JOURNAL ITEMS

1. Keep a record of the amount of time you spend watching television during an average week. Record what you watch and why you watch. Do your choices of programs reflect the uses and gratification formula?

2. How dangerous and mean do you think the world really is? How much television do you watch? Comment on the connection between the answers to these two questions.

3. Watch Saturday morning cartoons on a commercial television station. Record the number of violent incidents in 1 hour's programming. What are your comments on what you observe?

PANEL IDEAS

1. Invite a group of musicians or dee jays with various musical tastes (i.e., hip hop, country & western, pop, heavy metal, alternative, etc.) to discuss music with your class. Encourage students to be open to values of the music, despite some of the language that is violent and offensive to many people.

2. Ask the editor and several reporters for the campus newspaper to speak with your class. After introducing panelists, ask them questions such as 'How do you decide which stories to cover?' 'How do you decide which stories merit photos and how large photos are to be?' 'Do you have any policies governing language?'

DISCUSSION QUESTIONS

1. In reflecting on your own communication behaviors, do your relations with others rely predominantly on tribal, literate/print, or electronic means? Do you use different forms with different people? If so, why? In your own relationships, what is lost and what is gained by using each medium?

2. Bring three examples of advertisements from the media (e.g. newspapers, magazines, commercials) to class. Try to identify the prevailing ideologies in the ads. Who and what is privileged as the norm?

INTERNET WEB PAGE RESOURCES

Accuracy in Media
http://www.aim.org

Anti-Defamation League
http://www.adl.org

Association for Education in Journalism and Mass Communication
http://www.aejmc.org/

Association of Public Television Stations
http://www.apts.org

Cox Center for International Mass Communication and Training
http://www.grady.uga.edu/coxcenter/

Fairness & Accuracy In Reporting: The National Media Watch Group
http://www.fair.org

Freedom Forum-- Dedicated to Free Press, Free Speech and Free Spirit
http://www.freedomforum.org/

Media Ecology Association
http://www.media-ecology.org/

Media Research Center
http://www.mediaresearch.org

National Association of Broadcasters
http://www.nab.org/

National Press Club
http://npc.press.org/

National Public Radio
http://www.npr.org

Newspapers on the Net
http://www.onlinenewspapers.com/

Pew Research Center
http://www.people-press.org/

Public Relations Society of America
http://www.prsa.org/

Radio Station Locator
http://www.radio-locator.com/

Teaching Tolerance-- Southern Poverty Law Center
http://www.tolerance.org/index.jsp

Web Radio
http://www.web-radio.fm/

Chapter 14:
Technologies of Communication

I. There are many technologies of communication and more continue to be developed.
   A. Written communication was once the only way that people could exchange messages across distance.
       1. Memos, or memoranda, were once very popular in business; they are still used today.
       2. Written communication leaves a record and can protect us from misrepresentation.
       3. Memos and letters do have drawbacks.
           a. They take time and effort to prepare thoughtfully and logically using appropriate syntax, grammar, punctuation and spelling.
           b. Memos can be ignored in today's environment that gives more weight to the import of electronic messages.
           c. They cannot be transmitted as quickly and are more costly on an individual item basis.
   B. Telephones, and the fax as an extension of telephone technology, allow people to talk across distance.
   C. Computer-mediated communication is a major means of personal and business communication today.
       1. The Internet links people and databases around the world.
       2. Computer technologies have the advantage of speed in sending and receiving information.
       3. In the workplace, it has broken down the traditional patterns of needing to have all employees co-located in one place.
       4. People communicate differently on the net than when communicating face-to-face. Some claim it allows us to express ourselves more freely.
       5. Rules of etiquette for Email should be followed to make this means of communication effective.
       6. The Internet allows people to take control over parts of their lives that used to be controlled by government agencies and corporations.
   D. Teleconferencing allows 'meetings' among people who are geographically separated. It can take several forms.
       1. Audioconferencing allows people at different locations to talk together.
       2. Computer conferencing allows multiple participants to send and receive electronic mail and engage in a sequential discussion.
       3. Videoconferencing allows individuals to see and hear each other across distances, a major advantage over other kinds of teleconferencing.

E. New technologies are extensions and convergences of traditional forms of communication.
  1. Interconnectivity is the idea that various devices are connected to each other and to the net so that users don't need to worry about configuring each new system.
  2. In the future, each appliance or device that we use will have its own computer and be connected to the net.

II. New technologies of communication pose challenges.
  A. A major challenge is managing the flow of information in our lives.
    1. Many people feel overwhelmed by the sheer amount of information they receive each day.
    2. Information overload exists when we receive more information than we can manage effectively.
  B. There are two major ways in which computer usage tends to diminish our ability to stay focused on any one topic or activity.
    1. While multitasking, engaging in multiple tasks simultaneously or in overlapping ways, we are likely to do each one less well than if we concentrated on one.
    2. Computer use affects our attention through unequal stimulation of the right lobe of our brain, the one which specializes in artistic activity, as well as visual and spatial tasks, at the expense of the left lobe which deals with abstraction, as well as sequential and analytical thought.
  C. Another challenge of the information age is finding a way to cultivate the resources within us rather than continually relying on external stimulation.
  D. Ensuring democratic access to communication technologies is another important challenge.
    1. Some scholars claim technologies will encourage a 'global community' in which participation is not constrained by geographic location.
    2. Other scholars warn that new and converging technologies of communication will exacerbate social divisions: The haves will have access, and the have-nots will not.
  E. New and emerging technologies of communication challenge us to rethink what community means.
    1. Historically, community has been defined as a physical (geographically located) world made up of people who lived together and accommodated each other in order to sustain the collectivity.
    2. People linked together in cyberspace share no concrete physical location and don't need to accommodate each other as members of traditional communities did.
    3. People who communicate in cyberspace can deceive those with whom they communicate by suggesting that they are of a different ethnicity, age, gender, and so on.

F. New technologies challenge us to think about if and how they should be regulated, especially who should control the Internet and Web.
   1. Technologies of communication have developed quicker than we have been able to develop rules to safeguard people's health, privacy, comfort, and dignity.
   2. Companies such as Microsoft, which has tried to impose its proprietary standards on the industry, may be overstepping because no single private company had anything to do the development of the Internet and Web.
   3. The Internet and Web was developed by a partnership between universities and federal government.
   4. Many people are irritated by the excessive amount of advertising on the Internet.
   5. Privacy is a key issue that needs to be addressed.
   6. Many people assume that their online communication is private, but in reality hackers, company's employee monitoring systems, law enforcement agents, and others can access it.
   7. Court rulings so far have not supported privacy rights for on the job email and Web communicators.
   8. Some companies doing business on the net are endangering our health by not requiring prescriptions when they sell drugs to patients.

Vocabulary Terms

Audioconferencing

Avatars

Community

Cookies

Digital divide

Information

Information overload

Interconnectivity

Knowledge

Memoranda

Multitasking

Teleconferencing

Videoconferencing

ACTIVITY 14.1: Are You Sure That's True?

Purpose/Objective:
This activity will help you distinguish between credible online sources and sources lacking in credibility.

Instructions:
Select a communication related topic to research online. Identify three different web pages that are relevant to researching the topic, and then write a brief statement about each web page in which you clearly identify:

1. Communication topic (with reference page from the textbook).

2. URL: Location/address (URL) of the web page as well as its title.

3. Source: Source behind the web page (organization/person).

4. Credibility: Credibility of the source.

5. Summary: Brief summary of web page's contents.

6. Relevance: Relevance and usefulness of the web page to your research topic.

ACTIVITY 14.2: Researching with the Internet

Purpose/Objective:
This activity is designed to help you better understand the research process and sharpen your ability to screen out useless data from the Internet.

Instructions:
For this activity, you will need to use the Internet to "hunt down" as many of the following items as you can.

After each answer, indicate where you found the information, and state how you know what you've found is reliable.

1. The lyrics of a song that mentions the word "cat."

2. The scientific term for the nonverbal behavior of eye contact or pupil dilation.

3. A television program that features an Asian-American in a prominent role.

4. A recent newspaper article that references the phrase, "affirmative action."

5. A magazine article that provides a direct quote from the President of the United States.

6. A dramatic quotation (from a well known source).

7. A startling statistic regarding victims of crime.

8. The voting rate of Americans by ethnicity.

9. Current statistics on the number of part-time workers in the U. S.

10. An example of a television commercial that uses a female voice-over.

11. Women's annual income compared to men's (10 years ago and again, now).

12. The rate of marriage compared to the rate of divorce over the last decade.

13. The share of the population that is overweight—by sex.

14. Provide an expert statement of statistic about snack consumption in the U. S.

ACTIVITY 14.3: Tracking Information Flow

Purpose/Objective:
This exercise allows you to discover the kinds of communication technologies used by individuals in careers you might be considering for yourself.

Instructions:
Make an appointment with an individual who is in a career that you intend to enter or are considering entering. Interview the professional via e-mail, using the questions, below. These questions are just a guideline, so feel free to go beyond those.

After the interview, draw conclusions about information flow in the career you've selected. Contrast this against the information flow (or overflow) in your own life.

SURVEY OF COMMUNICATION TECHNOLOGY USE

1. On an average day, how much time do you spend sending and responding to electronic mail messages?

2. On an average day, how many fax messages do you send?

3. On an average day, how many fax messages do you receive?

4. On an average day, how much time do you spend on the World Wide Web?

5. On an average day, how much time do you spend working on-line?

6. On an average day, how many phone calls do you receive?

7. In an average week, in how many teleconferences do you participate?

8. In an average week, in how many video or computer conferences do you participate?

ACTIVITY 14.4: How Did You Know That About Me?

Purpose/Objective:
This exercise points out how easy it is to gain information about others, and how easily people can find out things about you.

Instructions:
Below are some concerns about access by others to information about you. According to the Privacy Rights Clearinghouse [http://www.privacyrights.org/fs/fs1-surv.htm], you should consider the following:

Check your credit report to find out if it contains any erroneous information.

People's medical histories are sometimes kept in insurance industry databases. Check with your health care provider to see if information about you is there.

Indicate to your bank that you do not want them to sell or share data about you with other companies.

Ask phone solicitors to remove you from their calling lists. Also, try to remove yourself from "junk" mailing lists.

Getting married or divorced, giving birth, selling your home, having a death in the family all generate public records of the event that others can access.

Do not share personal or financial information over the Internet. Anything you post can become public data unless encrypted or posted to a secure site.

If you call 800, 888, 877, 866, and 900 numbers your number might be recorded and sold and become part of a marketing list.

The signal of older model cordless phones can be intercepted.

ACTIVITY 14.5: Welcome To Our Family's Virtual Home

Purpose/Objective:
To gain practice in developing a website, and to build a stronger community among family members.

Instructions:
Check with your local Internet Service Provider, or with your school's technology department to see if they host web pages.

If so, build a web page that can serve as a repository for your family's memories, and as a community spot to promote communication among geographically dispersed members.

On the website, gather together and organize the following types of data:

Family stories and oral histories
Interviews with family members
The family genealogy
Photos
Streaming audio and video recordings
A directory for contacting family members
A threaded discussion board
Family recipes
A section just for kids
Vacation slides
Real-time web cam images

Be creative and solicit ideas from family members. This will help them feel like part of the process because they will have sense of ownership for the website.

ACTIVITY 14.6: Media Watch—Hollywood and Technology

Purpose/Objective:
This activity is intended to promote your critical reflection on converging technologies and their implications for how filmmakers tell their stories.

Instructions:
The merging of traditional film with computer technologies and particularly the use of Computer Generated Imagery (CGI) is changing the face of movies, television, and commercials. CGI is used to create props, models, miniature sets, elaborate backgrounds, and even characters (e.g., Woody in *Toy Story*). To get a better understanding of how filmed images of reality are quickly becoming almost anything the mind can imagine, visit the websites of some of the following studio/computer labs:

Prop-Art Ltd. [http://www.prop-art.com/]
Industrial Light and Magic [http://www.ilm.com/]
Dreamworks SKG [http://www.dreamworks.com/]

Review some of these older films that first began to use CGI in the late 1980s and early 1990s.
> *The Abyss*
> *Beauty and the Beast*
> *Terminator & Terminator 2*
> *The Nightmare Before Christmas*

Next, watch parts of the following films from the mid to late 1990s that furthered the use of CGI.
> *Toy Story*
> *Independence Day*
> *Star Wars: Episode I-The Phantom Menace*
> *The Mummy*

Finally, watch sections of recent films that have relied on heavy use of CGI.

> *The Mummy Returns*
> *Pearl Harbor*
> *Lord of the Rings*
> *Star Wars: Episode II-Attack of the Clones*
> *Shrek*

What conclusion can you draw about the possibilities of storytelling when visual communicators are no longer bound by physical realities? Will movies construct truly alternative realities for viewers? Do you think narratives will get better or will they be diminished as a result of form overpowering content?

JOURNAL ITEMS

1. Keep a log of your use of communication technologies for a three-day period. Record the amount of time you spend sending and receiving written communication, phone calls, and faxes. Also note the time you spend on the web, exchanging e-mail messages, and chatting on the Internet. What themes emerge when you analyze your log?

2. For one week, record the voice-mail messages you get from people who call you. Evaluate these messages using the rules for telephone etiquette presented in the textbook. During that same period, evaluate the messages you leave on answering machines of people you call.

PANEL IDEA

1. Invite two or more individuals at the cutting edge of communication technologies to speak with your class. Tell them you want them to enlarge the students' understandings of the current and future possibilities of new and converging technologies. Ask them to prepare informal remarks about what is now possible that is not yet widely used. Also ask them to offer their informed predictions about technologies that will be available in the near and less-near future.

   After the panelists speak for half of the period, invite students to ask questions. If necessary, prompt with some of your own prepared questions, such as: How will new technologies change family life? How will they transform our work—where and how we do it?

DISCUSSION QUESTIONS

1. For a 24-hour period, communicate with others only by computer (some nonverbal communication will be unavoidable). At the end of the period, reflect on whether you had a greater or diminished sense of connection with people. Was communication made easier or more difficult? What else did you experience? How did others react to you, and why? Were any communication technologies unavoidable? Why? Which technologies could you permanently do without? Which ones are indispensable for you? Why?

2. Break into groups to discuss the similarities and differences in nonverbal communication when interacting using e-mail, telephones/cell phones, beepers, face-to-face communication, written letters and postcards. How do nonverbal cues differ in the different contexts? How are relationships affected?

INTERNET WEB PAGE RESOURCES

Computer Professionals for Social Responsibility
http://www.cpsr.org/

Desktop Video Conferencing
http://www.coe.missouri.edu/~cjw/video/

E-Democracy
http://www.e-democracy.org/

Electronic Frontier Foundation
http://www.eff.org/

Electronic Privacy Information Center
http://www.epic.org

Institute for Global Communications
http://www.igc.org/

National Initiative for Democracy
http://nationalinitiative.org/

NetLingo The Internet Dictionary
http://www.netlingo.com/

New Luddites
http://www-users.york.ac.uk/~socs203/luddites.htm

Privacy.org
http://www.privacy.org

Search Engine Watch.com
http://searchenginewatch.com/

Society for Technical Communication
http://www.stc.org/

Webguardian
http://www.webguardian.com/

Website Users from Cultures Other than the U.S.
http://www.otal.umd.edu/uupractice/culture/

Virus Information
http://csrc.nist.gov/virus/

Appendix:
Communication in Interviews

I.   Interviews are communication transactions that emphasize questions and answers.

    A. Listening and speaking are equally important in interviewing.

    B. Eleven distinct types of interviews have been identified although often these kinds have multiple or conflicting purposes.

        1. Information-giving interviews provide information to another person.

        2. Information-getting interviews are used to gain information from people.

        3. Persuasive interviews are used to influence the attitudes or actions of others.

        4. Problem-solving interviews function to solve a problem collaboratively.

        5. Counseling interviews focus on helping one person (the interviewee) understand and deal with some problem.

        6. Employment interviews allow job candidates and employers to assess each other and the fit between them.

        7. Complaint interviews allow individuals to voice complaints about products, services, or individuals.

        8. Performance reviews are used to provide feedback to individuals on their performance.

        9. Reprimand interviews aim to identify problems in performance, determine causes of the problems, and generate a plan of improvement.

        10. Stress interviews are designed to create anxiety in interviewees in order to see how well interviewees manage stress.

        11. Exit interviews have the goal of gaining information, insights, and feedback about a place of work or education from a person who is leaving the organization.

II.   Interviews generally have a 3-part structure.

    A. The opening stage tends to be brief to create a good climate for the interview, clarify the purpose of the interview, and preview what will be covered.

    B. The substantive stage, which generally consumes the bulk of the time, focuses on the exchanging of information about issues relevant to the purpose of the interview.

        1. The substantive stage requires careful planning.

        2. The sequence of questions often follows the funnel sequence, moving from broad to narrow questions.

C. The closing stage, which tends to be brief, should summarize what has been communicated and state what follow-up, if any, will occur. It should also create parting good will.

III. Interviews have climates that shape the interaction.
    A. Interviewing styles vary in formality.
        1. Participants tend to stay closely to their social and professional roles in formal interviews as well as following a standard format.
        2. Informal interviews are more relaxed, flexible, and personal.
        3. Most interviews tend to fall between extremes of formality and informality.
    B. Interviewing styles vary in distribution of power between interviewer and interviewee.
        1. Mirror interviews reflect interviewees' comments. Interviewees can control the content of mirror interviews and therefore are the type in which they have the greatest power.
        2. Distributive interviews feature a relatively equal balance of power between interviewer and interviewee.
        3. In authoritarian interviews, the interviewer exerts primary control over the content and pace of communication.
        4. Stress interviews not only give the interviewer primary control, but also aim to create anxiety for the interviewee.

IV. Seven forms of questions are common in interviews.
    A. Open questions are broad queries that allow many kinds of answers.
    B. Closed questions call for specific and brief responses.
    C. Mirror questions reflect off previous communication.
    D. Hypothetical questions ask individuals to respond to speculative situations.
    E. Probing questions go beneath the surface of a response to dig for more information.
    F. Leading questions (loaded questions) slant responses in a specific direction.
    G. Summary questions cover what has been discussed and allow the respondent to correct or amplify the summary.

V. There are two specific challenges for effective communication in interviews.
    A. Preparing for interviews is essential for effectiveness.
        1. Researching the topics, participants, and the context of the discussion prior to the interview is important.
            a. Being well informed enhances your credibility.
            b. Knowing something about the interview topic in advance helps you to adapt your communication to the norms and expectations of the interviewer.
        2. Person-centered communication during interviews promotes effectiveness.

3. Practicing responding allows interviewees to refine their answers and styles of communicating.

B. Managing illegal questions is a challenge in some interviews.

   1. Both interviewers and interviewees should be aware of laws and more specific policies that regulate what can and cannot be asked during interviews.

   2. In advance of an interview, an interviewee should consider how she or he will respond if an illegal question is posed.

Vocabulary Terms

Authoritarian interview

Closed questions

Complaint interview

Counseling interview

Distributive interview

Employment interview

Exit interview

Funnel sequence

Hypothetical questions

Information-getting interview

Information-giving interview

Interview

Leading questions

Mirror interview

Mirror questions

Performance review

Persuasive interview

Probing questions

Problem-solving interview

Reprimand interview

Stress interview

Summary questions

ACTIVITY A.1: Rephrasing Illegal, Negative, & Loaded Questions

Purpose/Objective:
This exercise is designed to help you learn ways to avoid negative, loaded, or illegal (according to the EEOC) questions

Instructions:
Below is a list of negatively worded or loaded questions. Assume for a moment that your are interviewing for a job that for which you ate very interested. Think about how you could best answer each of the following questions.

A. Are you planning on having any more children?

B. Are you a native speaker of English?

C. Are you physically disabled?

D. Have you ever been convicted of a felony?

E. How old are you?

F. Are you married/do you intend to marry?

G. Have you seen a therapist?

H. Do you own a car?

I. Do you own a house?

J. What is your political affiliation?

K. Are you a socialist?

L. May I have a picture of you to put in your file?

M. Does your religion allow you to work on Saturdays?

N. Would you be willing to live in a town without a church, synagogue, or temple?

O. Do you have reliable childcare?

ACTIVITY A.2: Can I Ask You a Few Questions?

Purpose/Objective:
This activity should allow you to apply what they have read about different interviewing styles and to see how each style shapes what happens in interviews.

Instructions:
Find three friends or family members who are willing to let you interview them about some aspect of their lives. For each person, arrange a date, time, and place where the two of you will not be interrupted.

Prior to the interview, develop a set of questions based on one of the following three interviewing styles:

Mirror
Distributive
Authoritarian

After you have completed all three interviews, reflect on what differences you experienced among them. With which style did you feel most comfortable? Which interviewee seemed the most at ease? In what situations would the different types of interviews be most appropriate?

ACTIVITY A.3: I'm Glad You Asked That

Purpose/Objective:
This activity will allow you to closely study the nature and structure of questions a professional interviewer uses to elicit information from an interviewee.

Instructions:
Locate the transcript of an extended interview conducted by a news journalist talk with someone noteworthy.

Identify the opening stage of the interview, and focus on how the interviewee transitions into the substantive stage. Likewise, search for the transition that the journalist uses to signal a move toward the closing stage of the interview.

Using different colored pens, mark leading questions, probing questions, and hypothetical questions. Also make different notations next to open ended and closed ended questions.

Assess the text in terms of the relationship between the interviewer and the interviewee. Does the journalist employ a mirror style, distributive style, authoritarian style, or a stress approach?

Finally, what questions would you have asked, or what responses would you have followed up on, that the journalist neglected to ask?

ACTIVITY A.4: Forming Questions

Purpose/Objective:
This activity gives you a chance to become familiar with different forms of questions and to appreciate how each is constructed.

Instructions:
For each of the following three topics, develop the kinds of question specified.

1. You want to know why an applicant to your school is interested in enrolling.

A. Open question:

B. Closed question:

C. Probing question:

D. Leading question:

E. Mirror question:

F. Hypothetical question:

2. You want to help the interviewee think through whether he/she would enjoy belonging to a Greek organization on campus.

A. Open question:

B. Hypothetical question:

C. Closed question:

3. You need to tell the interviewee that her or his performance on a job has been unsatisfactory and explore how to improve her or his performance.

A. Closed question:

B. Leading question:

C. Probing question:

D. Summary question:

ACTIVITY A.5: Do You Remember When?

Purpose/Objective:
This activity will give you practice in research skills, a chance to develop a list of interview questions, and the opportunity to speak with several strangers.

Instructions:
Look through the archives of the local newspaper, starting 50 years ago. For each decade, identify a couple of major events that occurred and that the town's people are likely to remember. Develop a list of interview questions for each of the events.

Next, locate a person who remembers one of the events and is willing to be interviewed about the subject. Set up an interview with them and gather their recollections. Continue to interview people until you have at least one person for each decade.

Ask the interviewees if they mind having their interviews publishes. If they grant you permission, collect the interviews into a single story and offer it to the town's newspaper for possible publication as a feature story about what people have undergone in the town over the last fifty years.

You might also consider binding the text of the interview together and donating it to the local history museum, which may contain a compilation of oral histories.

ACTIVITY A.6: Media Watch—It's Late Night With...

Purpose/Objective:
This activity will help you focus on the interviewing techniques used to solicit entertaining information from others.

Instructions:
Videotape a couple of the late-night talk shows in order to analyze the style and techniques the interviewer uses to elicit colorful stories from his or her guest.

In particular, try to identify the opening stage, the substantive stage and the closing stage of the interview. Are questions mostly open ended or closed ended?

What seems to be the balance of power between program's host and the guests? Does this seem to manifest itself in the form of "mirror" interviews, "distributive" interviews, "authoritarian" interviews, or "stress" interviews? Why do you suppose this is the case?

Are leading, probing and or hypothetical questions evident? How effectively are these used, if they are present?

Overall, how would you judge the quality of the interviewer? Why?

JOURNAL ITEMS

1. Make an appointment to interview someone who interests you. It might be a professor whose teaching engages you, or a professional in a career that interests you. Prepare for the interview by writing out questions of different types. Some of your questions should be open, some closed, some leading, and so forth. During the interview, note how the type of question you pose affects the length and content of response.

2. Go to the career or placement center at your school. Conduct research on one company or graduate school that interests you. What did you learn about the company or school that you didn't know before your research?

PANEL IDEA

1. Invite one or more members of staff at the campus placement center to speak with your class. Ask the individual(s) to prepare a one-class period workshop on how to interview effectively. Encourage the speaker(s) to involve the students in role-playing and other activities that allow them to practice skills.

DISCUSSION QUESTIONS

1. Think about a job that you would like to have after graduating from college. Describe how you would prepare for an employment interview with an employer in that field.

2. Recount a time when you were interviewed. What was the type of interview (i.e., employment, complaining, counseling, etc.)? Do you think the interviewer was well prepared and did a good job? Why or why not? Were you satisfied with your responses? What, if anything, would you change about the interview?

INTERNET WEB PAGE RESOURCES

Career Journal of the Wall Street Journal
http://www.careerjournal.com/jobhunting/interviewing

Effective Interviewing: The Virtual Interviewing Assistant
http://www.ukans.edu/cwis/units/coms2/via/index.html

Human Resources Web Guide: Employee Interviewing and Selection
http://www.bsad.uvm.edu/hrm/selection/selectionhome.htm

Interviewing Information
http://www.collegegrad.com/intv/index.shtml

Legal and Illegal Interview Questions
http://www.usfca.edu/fac-staff/bell/article18.html

Monster Jobs
http://www.monster.com/

U.S. Equal Employment Opportunity Commission
http://www.eeoc.gov/

Video Interviews
http://www.careerjournal.com/jobhunting/interviewing/20011011-rosemarin.html

Self-Test for Chapter 1
The Field of Communication

Multiple Choice

1. The field of communication is how old?
   a. 1000 years
   b. over 2500 years
   c. 50 years
   d. 100 years

2. In ancient Greece, communication education focused on:
   a. Effective group discussion
   b. Public speaking (rhetoric)
   c. Parliamentary procedure
   d. None of the above

3. The many areas in the field of communication are unified by which central theme(s)?
   a. Feedback and symbols
   b. Symbols and meaning
   c. Noise and feedback
   d. Messages and noise

4. The most sophisticated models of communication are:
   a. Linear and Interactive
   b. Interactive and Multiplied
   c. Pluralistic and Multiplied
   d. Interactive and Transactive

5. Which of the following is NOT true of communication, as presented in this textbook?
   a. Communication utilizes symbols.
   b. Communication involves meanings.
   c. Communication is static.
   d. Communication is systemic.

6. At one time, rhetoric was:
   a. Practiced only by licensed professional, trained in England and Scotland
   b. Seen as a practical art for public speaking

     c. Taught as an important part of the scientific method

     d. Limited to people studying interpersonal relationships

7. In organizations, employees generally have shared understandings of their organization's goals and values as well as appropriate codes of conduct on the job. These shared understandings are called:

     a. Organizational themes

     b. Work life codes

     c. Organizational culture

     d. Professional etiquette

8. Which of the following is NOT one of the basic communication processes discussed in the textbook?

     a. Engaging in verbal communication

     b. Creating interaction climates

     c. Engaging in self-disclosure

     d. Listening and responding

9. Textual analysis is a form of which research approach?

     a. Quantitative

     b. Critical

     c. Qualitative

     d. Analytical

10. The interactive model of communication extended the linear model through the addition of:

     a. Feedback

     b. Noise

     c. Encoding

     d. Redundancy

True/False

_____ 1. In intimate relationships, the primary values of communication are problem solving and self-disclosure.

_____ 2. Communication Scholars use their research to develop new theories and raise social awareness

_____ 3. Linear models of communication emphasized feedback between communicators.

_____ 4. Concern with ethics is separated from other specific areas in the field of communication.

_____ 5. Symbols are central to all forms of communication.

Essays

1. Describe the relationships between communication and personal life. Your essays should discuss both the role of communication in shaping identity and the values of communication to individuals.

2. Describe the five of the ten areas of interest in the modern field of communication.

Self-Test for Chapter 2
Perceiving and Understanding

Multiple Choice

1. Which of the following is NOT a dimension of attributions?
   a. Internal/external locus
   b. Stable/unstable
   c. Organized/disorganized
   d. Global/specific

2. Grant says, 'I didn't get the job, but it wasn't because I messed up the interview. The interviewer asked really difficult questions and all of my preparation couldn't have prepared me.' Grant's explanation for not getting the job illustrates
   a. Self-fulfilling prophecy
   b. Self-serving bias
   c. The influence of social roles
   d. Cultural sense making

3. 'Dr. Friedrich is the best professor I ever had.' In this statement, Dr. Friedrich is a(n):
   a. Prototype
   b. Stereotype
   c. Personal construct
   d. Script

4. 'Dr. Friedrich is more informed and interesting than other professors I've had.' In this statement, Dr. Friedrich is perceived using which form of schemata?
   a. Prototypes
   b. Personal constructs
   c. Stereotypes
   d. Scripts

5. In contrast to couples that are unhappy, happy couples tend to attribute nice things a partner does to:
   a. Stable, specific, internal causes
   b. Unstable, global, external causes
   c. Stable, global, internal causes
   d. Stable, global, external causes

6. Cognitive complexity is demonstrated by which of the following statements:
   a. 'We need to be flexible in how we view the problem.'
   b. 'There are too many options to consider. Let's pick the most obvious one.'
   c. 'People follow the path of least resistance.'
   d. 'Right is right and wrong is wrong.'

7. According to standpoint theory:
   a. Cultures include different social groups that have equal power
   b. Different social groups in a culture have distinct degrees of power
   c. Standpoints affect how individuals perceive the world
   d. A, B, and C

8. Marcia assumes her roommate will not be willing to discuss a personal problem, so Marcia doesn't bring the problem up. Marcia has engaged in:
   a. Mind reading
   b. Static evaluation
   c. Polarized thinking
   d. Empathy

9. Don sees a person stumbling out of a local bar and Don says to himself, 'that dude is drunk as a skunk.' Don has failed to distinguish between:
   a. Perception and interpretation
   b. Prototypes and scripts
   c. Facts and inferences
   d. Empathy and person-perception

10. All of the following are interrelated elements of the perception process EXCEPT:
    a. Selection
    b. Interpretation
    c. Attribution
    d. Organization

True/False

_____ 1. Perception is the passive process of receiving and interpreting data.
_____ 2. Prototypes are bi-polar mental yardsticks.
_____ 3. People who are cognitively complex tend to be less person-centered than people who are less cognitively complex.
_____ 4. North American culture is highly individualistic.
_____ 5. Empathy is the ability to feel precisely what another person feels.

Essays

1. Define mindreading and discuss its appropriateness in interpersonal communication.

2. Explain the relationship between self-serving bias and internal/external attributions. Give an example of a statement that shows self-serving bias and discuss the dangers of such statements.

Self-Test for Chapter 3
Creating Communication Climates

Multiple Choice

1. Andy tends to openly judge and evaluate the ideas and statements expressed by his associates and friends. This tends to make others feel:
    a. Comfortable
    b. Judgmental
    c. Positive
    d. Defensive

2. Brian is convinced that he always has the right answer to every situation. This form of communication would be termed:
    a. Provisional
    b. Certainty
    c. Disruptive
    d. Descriptive

3. Mary prefers to be straightforward when asking for a favor rather that prefacing her request by reciting all the favors she has done for you in the past. Her communication is _____ than strategic:
    a. Spontaneous
    b. Certain
    c. Evaluative
    d. Ethnocentric

4. Typically neutral communication:
    a. Implies indifference
    b. Is a sign of a lack of empathy
    c. May be interpreted as disconfirming
    d. All of the above

5. When his friend Bob comes into his room, Will looks up and says, 'Hi, dude.' This is an example of which of the following levels of confirmation?
    a. Recognition
    b. Acknowledgment
    c. Endorsement
    d. Equality

6. Bob tells Will about a problem he has and Will responds by saying, 'Your analysis of the problem is very sound. I would feel just like you do.' This response illustrates which level of confirmation?
    a. Recognition
    b. Acknowledgment
    c. Endorsement

     d. Equality

7. When interacting with a person who has a severe visual impairment, which of the following is (are) good guidelines?
     a. Avoid phrases such as 'see you later.'
     b. In groups preface comments to the visually impaired person with her or his name.
     c. Speak to the person's companion or interpreter rather than directly to the person with the visual impairment.
     d. A, B, and C

8. Rob and Lisa discover they have a strong difference of opinion when they discuss a job offer Rob got that would require them to move. When Rob says he wants to take the offer, Lisa walks out. This exemplifies which response to conflict?
     a. Exit
     b. Voice
     c. Loyalty
     d. Neglect

9. Rob decides not to push things but to just remain quietly committed to Lisa and to hope their disagreement blows over. This exemplifies which response to conflict?
     a. Exit
     b. Voice
     c. Loyalty
     d. Neglect

10. A person who sees a disagreement as a battle that can only have one victor is known as a _____ orientation:
     a. Win- win
     b. Lose- Lose
     c. Win- lose
     d. Constructive

True/False

_____ 1. Research has shown that for the most part people would rather have friends not be honest with their feedback if the content is unpleasant.
_____ 2. The highest level of confirmation is acknowledgment.
_____ 3. Strategic communication aims to manipulate by keeping motives and/or intentions hidden.
_____ 4. Descriptive communication fosters a more defensive climate.
_____ 5. Covert conflict is more difficult to resolve than overt conflict.

Essays

1. Identify and describe the specific kinds of communication that tend to foster defensive and supportive communication climates. Provide specific examples of each.
2. Describe and explain the four responses to conflict. Provide examples for each.

Self-Test for Chapter 4
Engaging in Verbal Communication

Multiple Choice

1. Symbols are:
   a. Arbitrary
   b. Ambiguous
   c. Abstract
   d. All of the above

2. Which of the following terms is the LEAST abstract?
   a. President of the United States
   b. Citizen of Pittsburgh
   c. Man
   d. person

3. 'Do not interrupt when others are speaking.' This is an example of a(n):
   a. Constitutive rule
   b. Regulative rule
   c. Punctuation
   d. Abstraction

4. 'Paying attention when others speak is a sign of respect.' This is an example of a(n):
   a. Constitutive rule
   b. Regulative rule
   c. Punctuation
   d. Abstraction

5. When we overlook many aspects of a person and define the person only by a single aspect of her or his identity, we are:
   a. Organizing
   b. Engaging in dual perspective
   c. Totalizing
   d. Stereotyping

6. The possibility of misunderstanding between people:
   a. Increases as language becomes less abstract
   b. Increases as language becomes more abstract
   c. Decreases when language is not symbolic
   d. Decreases when we use you-language

7. 'When I get out of school, I want to go to France.' This is an example of:
   a. Using symbols to define
   b. Using symbols to organize

    c. Engaging in hypothetical thought
    d. Engaging in punctuation

8. 'All people who go to private schools are snobs.' This statement is an example of:
    a. Stereotyping
    b. Hypothesizing
    c. Using I-language
    d. Self-reflecting

9. The I aspect of self is:
    a. Socially aware
    b. Sensitive to social norms
    c. Impulsive
    d. A and B

10. The ability to consciously think in all three dimensions of time arises because human beings can:
    a. Think hypothetically
    b. Use I-language
    c. Think indexically
    d. Qualify language

True/False

_____ 1. All symbols have objective concrete meanings.
_____ 2. Static evaluations focus only on what is negative about a person.
_____ 3. Punctuating verbal communication places the flow of conversation into meaningful units.
_____ 4. Interpretation is a subjective process.
_____ 5. Indexing is a way to increase the abstractness that is inherent in language.

Essays

1. Explain why symbols allow human beings to live, think, and feel in ways that would not be possible if we were not symbol users.

2. Define I-language and You-language, and provide concrete examples of each. Explain the values of using I-language.

Self-Test for Chapter 5
Engaging in Nonverbal Communication

Multiple Choice

1. The three dimensions of relational-level meanings that may be expressed nonverbally are:
    a. Power, control, and liking
    b. Power, liking, and disliking
    c. Power, liking, and responsiveness
    d. Liking, responsiveness, and disliking

2. Kinesics refers to:
    a. Touching and being touched
    b. Body position and motion
    c. Environmental features that affect interaction
    d. Personal space

3. Estimations are that nonverbal communication accounts for what range of total communication?
    a. Between 20 to 30%
    b. Between 80 to 90%
    c. Between 65 to 93%
    d. Between 52 to 75%

4. Scott makes it a point to sit as close as possible to individuals with high status. Scott's choice of seating position is an example of:
    a. Chronemics
    b. Proxemics
    c. Paralanguage
    d. Kinesics

5. Views of what is an attractive weight in women are influenced by:
    a. Socioeconomic class
    b. Race and ethnicity
    c. Age
    d. A and B

6. The first sense to develop in human beings is:
    a. Sight
    b. Smell
    c. Touch
    d. Hearing

7. The CEO always keeps others waiting for 10 minutes at meetings. She has the power to be late, whereas others don't and they will wait. This illustrates:

a. Chronemics
b. Proxemics
c. Paralanguage
d. Kinesics

8. Gil invites his girlfriend Nancy to go to his home and meet his parents. When in his home, Nancy notices a lot of high quality silverware and imported rugs and sees pictures of the family on cruise ships and at resorts. Nancy concludes that Gil's family is wealthy. Her conclusion is based on:
   a. Haptics
   b. Proxemics
   c. Artifacts
   d. Chronemics

9. In giving an exam review, Professor Sparks says, 'The MOST important thing to know is…' and uses greater volume when saying 'most.' This illustrates using which nonverbal behavior to reinforce the verbal message?
   a. Haptics
   b. Paralanguage
   c. Chronemics
   d. Kinesics

10. Gus' is a very popular fast food diner. To get customers served and on their way as quickly as possible the most successful environmental factor that the owner of Gus' should consider is (are):
    a. Play relaxing and subdued music
    b. Have soft, upholstered chairs for some customers
    c. Have bright lights and hard booths
    d. All of the above

True/False

_____ 1. Nonverbal communication reflects cultural values.
_____ 2. People with high status are more likely to touch people with less status than vice versa.
_____ 3. Silence can convey either contentment or contempt.
_____ 4. Haptics refers to we perceive and use time.
_____ 5. Vocal volume is a form of paralanguage.

Essays

1. Design an environment that encourages relaxed, friendly interaction among people. Explain decisions you make about nonverbal features of the environment that you intend to contribute to the relaxed atmosphere.

2. A friend tells you that he just bought a book titled 'Read Anyone's Nonverbal Communication with 100% Accuracy' and that he intends to break the 'hidden code' of communication. Based on your study of nonverbal communication, what advice would you give to your friend?

Self-Test for Chapter 6
Listening and Responding to Others

Multiple Choice

1. Keith feels overwhelmed by communication coming from people at a meeting he attends. While the Chair is talking about the task of the group, members are engaged in sideline conversations, and computer graphics are being presented— all at the same time. Keith is experiencing:
   a. Message complexity
   b. Preoccupation
   c. Message overload
   d. Prejudgment

2. Beth goes to a public presentation by an author whose work she has read and of which she disapproves. Before the author begins speaking, Beth thinks to herself, 'I know what he's going to say and I know he is wrong.' Beth's ability to listen effectively is likely to be hampered by:
   a. Message complexity
   b. Preoccupation
   c. Message overload
   d. Prejudgment

3. Nathan listens carefully to what his father says in order to refute his father's ideas. As soon as his father pauses, Nathan jumps in and says, 'You said three things that don't stand up.' Nathan seems to be engaging in:
   a. Ambushing
   b. Defensive listening
   c. Monopolizing
   d. Pseudolistening

4. Mary is trying to do some last minute cramming before an exam. So, while she is sitting in her psychology class, she is reading over her notes for the upcoming research methods exam. Mary looks up at the psychology professor often and nods her head to indicate she is attentive. Mary is engaging in:
   a. Ambushing
   b. Defensive listening
   c. Monopolizing
   d. Pseudolistening

5. While his friend Kevin is speaking, Ray interjects these comments: 'go on,' 'I'm following you,' 'what happened next?' These are examples of:
   a. Showing dual perspective
   b. Expressing support
   c. Minimal encouragers
   d. Paraphrasings

6. Research cited in the text indicates that after about 8 hours most people forget about how much of what they hear?
    a. One third
    b. Two thirds
    c. One half
    d. 90%

7. All BUT ONE of the following would be appropriate techniques for becoming a more effective critical listener:
    a. Listening carefully so to find flaws and deceptions in the speaker's communication
    b. Attempt to minimize distractions
    c. Ask questions that allows the speaker to clarify and/or elaborate
    d. Repeat new ideas to yourself immediately after hearing them

8. Which of the following is NOT an internal obstacle to effective listening?
    a. Prejudgments
    b. Message complexity
    c. Lack of effort
    d. Preoccupation

9. To help herself remember a lecture, Sharlene makes up a word in which each letter represents a key idea from the lecture. The word Sharlene makes up is called a:
    a. Mnemonic
    b. Memorabilia
    c. Retendo
    d. Pneumatic device

10. Steve is suspicious that his computer is not working properly. He cuts off all other noise and listens to the computer as he gives it commands. He hears a whirring sound that has not been present before and decides to take the machine in for a tune-up. Steve was listening:
    a. For pleasure
    b. Critically
    c. To discriminate
    d. For information

True/False

_____ 1. Listening is physiological activity that occurs when sound waves strike functional eardrums.
_____ 2. There appears to be no gender differences in how people listen.
_____ 3. Mindfulness is the foundation of listening for pleasure, for information, and to support others.

_____ 4. We listen on two levels, the content level and the relationship level.

_____ 5. When we focus on only particular parts of the communication we are engaging in defensive listening.

Essays

1. Describe the attitudes and skills that are particularly useful when the goal of listening is to support others.

2. Choose a form of ineffective listening, and describe and explain it as well as providing some hypothetical examples.

Self-Test for Chapter 7
Adapting Communication to People and Contexts

Multiple Choice

1. Groups that live in a dominant culture and also belong to another culture are now termed:
   a. Nomads
   b. Social communities
   c. Subcultures
   d. Dual cultures

2. Which of the following affects how communication systems operate, what it means, and what will be effective communication?
   a. Understanding
   b. Tolerance
   c. Participation
   d. Context

3. The extent to which a system affects and is affected by outside processes and factors is known as:
   a. Openness
   b. Homeostasis
   c. Culture
   d. Standpoint

4. Masculine socialization places more emphasis on:
   a. Using communication as an end in and of itself
   b. Using communication to cement relationships
   c. Using communication instrumentally
   d. Supportive listening

5. Research suggests that African American culture generally communicates more _____ than European Americans:
   a. Authentically
   b. Respectfully
   c. Effectively
   d. Assertively

6. Our experiences as members of a particular social group shape the way we perceive the world and ourselves, and the ways we communicate is the central premise of:
   a. Standpoint theory
   b. Cultural theory
   c. Social group theory
   d. Differentiation theory

7. Views of what is good, right, and worthwhile that are shared among members of a culture is called:
   a. Standards
   b. Values
   c. Morality
   d. Properties

8. Although socialized in a masculine climate to be analytical and competitive, Gus gradually learns to understand his long time girlfriend's ways of feminine communication style. Some communication theorists suggest Gus has become:
   a. Univocal
   b. Multilingual
   c. Feminized
   d. Subordinated

9. The tendency to think one's own culture is superior to other cultures is called:
   a. Egocentrism
   b. Cultural relativism
   c. Moral relativism
   d. Ethnocentrism

10. Dan thinks women's communication style is ineffective, but he accepts the fact that they do have their own ways of communicating. Dan's response to women's communication illustrates:
    a. Resistance
    b. Toleration
    c. Understanding
    d. Assimilation

True/False

_____ 1. Geographic boundaries define cultures.
_____ 2. Cultural relativism is the same as moral relativism.
_____ 3. Members of a culture may give up their native ways and adopt those of a different culture.
_____ 4. Multiple cultures may co-exist within a single society.
_____ 5. Cultures are systems.

Essays

1. Compare and contrast ethnocentric bias and cultural relativism. Provide concrete examples of each.

2. Identify and describe five different ways of responding to cultural diversity. Include concrete examples in your discussion.

Self-Test for Chapter 8
Communication and Personal Identity

Multiple Choice

1. Keith says to his son, Nathan, 'You're a big boy and you can do this yourself.' This is an example of:
    a. Reflected appraisal
    b. Self-sabotage
    c. Direct definition
    d. Attachment style

2. Keith is consistently loving and responsive to Nathan when they interact. This suggests that Nathan is experiencing which attachment style?
    a. Dismissive
    b. Anxious/ambivalent
    c. Ambivalent
    d. Secure

3. Nathan says, 'My friend's says I am strong, so I must be strong.' Nathan's comment illustrates:
    a. Self sabotage
    b. Identity script
    c. Reflected appraisal
    d. Social comparison

4. Nathan plays ball with his friends and realizes that he can hit better than they can. Nathan thinks, 'I really am a good hitter.' Nathan's reassessment of his batting ability is prompted by:
    a. Social comparison
    b. Direct definition
    c. Self-sabotage
    d. Reflected appraisal

5. Modern day Western culture emphasizes _____ as central to personal identity.
    a. Race
    b. Sex
    c. National heritage
    d. All of the above

6. The general views and values endorsed by a society or social group are called:
    a. The perspective of particular others
    b. Self-fulfilling prophecy
    c. The perspective of the generalized other
    d. Identity scripts

7. Bill's parents continuously tell him, 'you can't trust others,' 'look out for yourself because no one else will,' and 'don't believe what people tell you.' The rules for living and identity that Bill is acquiring from his family are known as:
    a. Self-fulfilling prophecies
    b. Identity scripts
    c. Definitional identities
    d. Familial schematics

8. Kate's co-workers perceive her as a natural leader but Kate doesn't recognize this quality in herself. The Joahri Window would place this information in Kate's _____ area.
    a. Free
    b. Unknown
    c. Blind
    d. Detached

9. Adam and Jean are in the early stages of a new relationship. Adam feels that to enhance closeness and develop an intimate relationship with Jean he should:
    a. Advocate novel activities with her so he can learn how she reacts
    b. Compare how other couples in the same stage of relationship are behaving
    c. Disclose little about himself until the relationship appears secured
    d. Self-disclose gradually and cautiously, but resolutely as reciprocated

10. Whenever Marie sees Laurel, Laurel smiles and says something nice about how Marie looks or what she is doing. As a result, Marie always feels better about herself when she's around Laurel. For Marie, Laurel is a(n):
    a. Downer
    b. Generalized other
    c. Upper
    d. Attachment style

True/False

_____1. Humans have selves at birth.

_____2. Tolerance for sexual orientation interacts with socioeconomic level.

_____3. Particular others are those institutions which exhibit specific roles, rules and values endorsed by the social community in which we live.

_____4. Downers are other people who communicate negatively about us about our self worth.

_____5. One of the best ways to seek personal growth as a communicator is to set high, and hypothetical, goals.

Essays

1. Describe how supportive contexts can create a climate for growth and change. Discuss and provide examples, of those people who both nourish or impede this process.

2. Describe and differentiate between particular others and the generalized other. Give examples of each.

Self-Test for Chapter 9
Communication in Personal Relationships

Multiple Choice

1. Cindy and Charlie feel torn between liking their comfortable routines and wanting more spontaneity in their relationship. They are experiencing tension from which relational dialectic?
   a. Autonomy/connectedness
   b. Novelty/predictability
   c. Openness/closedness
   d. Structure/flexibility

2. To deal with the tension they feel, Cindy and Charlie decide to focus more being spontaneous even if it means suppressing the comfort they achieve from routinization. This illustrates which response to relational dialectics?
   a. Neutralization
   b. Separation
   c. Segmentation
   d. Reframing

3. Cindy and Charlie then discover they are uncomfortable having so much uncertainty. They then decide that maybe they should just settle into their routines and not try to inject novelty into their relationship. This illustrates which response to relational dialectics?
   a. Neutralization
   b. Separation
   c. Segmentation
   d. Reframing

4. The benchmark of established, stabilized friendships is:
   a. The assumption of increasing involvement
   b. The displacement of social norms and roles with personal values and standards
   c. The assumption of continuity
   d. The anticipation and desire for more closeness

5. Kevin sees love relationships as a challenging game and remains unsure of his own desires or his partners commitment. His style of loving is best described as:
   a. Ludic
   b. Manic
   c. Erotic
   d. Agapic

6. Eddie believes that true love grows gradually to eventually create an even-kneeled companionship. Eddie's style of loving is best described as:

a. Pragma
b. Storge
c. Erotic
d. Agapic

7. Among the greatest problems reported by partners in long-distance relationships is (are):
    a. Not being able to share small talk and daily routines
    b. Unrealistic expectations for time together
    c. Inability to share major events with each other
    d. A and B

8. The phase of relational breakdown marked by figuring out how to explain the breakup is the:
    a. Social phase
    b. Dyadic phase
    c. Intrapsychic phase
    d. Interpersonal phase

9. The most egalitarian relationships in terms of shared homemaking and child care are more likely to be found in:
    a. Heterosexual marriages
    b. Heterosexual cohabitation
    c. Gay commitments
    d. Lesbian commitments

10. Friendship begins with:
    a. Friendly relations
    b. Stepping out of social roles
    c. Role-limited interactions
    d. Disclosing feelings, values, goals and attitudes

True/False

_____1. Social relationships are commitments between individuals who are irreplaceable.

_____2. Passion is the primary foundation for enduring relationships.

_____3. Regulative rules in relationships define what various kinds of communication means.

_____4. Proximity influences attraction.

_____5. Violence and abuse in intimate relationships seldom stops without intervention.

Essays

1. Describe the problems inherent in geographic separation for friends or romantic couples. Provide specific examples for each situation and offer some realistic solutions to overcome these.

2. Describe the stages in friendship. Include concrete examples of each stage.

Self-Test for Chapter 10
Communication in Groups and Teams

Multiple Choice

1. Which of the following is NOT a characteristic of small groups?
    a. Common goals
    b. Independence among members
    c. Shared rules of conduct
    d. Interaction over time

2. Potential limitations of small groups in comparison to individuals include:
    a. Time required
    b. Cohesion
    c. Conformity pressures
    d. A and C

3. The special energy in groups that is more than the additive energy of members is called:
    a. Synergy
    b. Cohesion
    c. Commitment
    d. Groupthink

4. Group Z has worked together for a long time and a level of cohesion and group spirit exists among members. Over time the members have come to perceive their group so positively they assume they cannot make bad decisions and stifle those who attempt to raise challenges. This group seems to be experiencing:
    a. Decision-making malaise
    b. Power
    c. Task commitment
    d. Groupthink

5. In her group, Grace realizes that Tom is the most important member. Tom has a close relationship with the company president and can make or break individuals' careers. Grace works to win Tom's notice and support of her. Grace is engaging in:
    a. Centralizing power
    b. Social climbing
    c. Power to
    d. Individualism

6. Robert Knight, the chair of the university's athletic compliance committee, provides performance reviews on all of the group's members as well as having the authority to assign members particularly high status positions. Mr. Knight is considered to hold:

a. Authorized power
b. Power to
c. Power over
d. Leadership

7. Charlene repeatedly takes up group time to talk about personal issues, especially problems, in her life. This kind of communication is:
   a. Procedural
   b. Task
   c. Climate
   d. Egocentric

8. Susan, a member of Charlene's group, says, 'Maybe you and I could talk about your personal concerns after our group meeting so that we can stay on schedule now.' This is an example of:
   a. Procedural communication
   b. Task communication
   c. Dialectical communication
   d. Egocentric communication

9. Communication that initiates ideas, seeks information, and evaluates ideas is called:
   a. Procedural
   b. Task
   c. Climate
   d. Egocentric

10. Dr. Fritz, the college's communication department's chairperson, assigns five faculty members to review, evaluate and provide recommendations on the future direction of the department's curriculum. Dr. Fritz has assembled what type of group?
    a. Procedural
    b. Advisory
    c. Quality
    d. Focus

True/False

_____1. All groups are teams.
_____2. All teams are groups
_____3. The ideal size for a small group is 5 to 7 members
_____4. Decentralized patterns of interaction promote balanced communication.
_____5. Quality circles are tasked to make concessions.

Essays

1. Discuss leadership, what it is, what it does, and how it operates within a group that has multiple leaders.

2. Identify, discuss, and provide examples of important potential strengths of groups in comparison to individuals.

Self-Test for Chapter 11
Communication in Organizations

Multiple Choice

1. Shortly after David joins a company, his co-worker tells him: 'Watch out for Cindy. She'll be nice to you and then stab you in the back.' This is an example of a(n):
   a. Collegial story
   b. Personal story
   c. Corporate story
   d. Enhancement rite.

2. On your first day at work, your supervisor stops by and says, 'Around here, we prize initiative. The man who founded this company 48 years ago, struck out on his own, and took big risks. That's who we are.' This is an example of a(n):
   a. Collegial story
   b. Personal story
   c. Corporate story
   d. Enhancement rite.

3. The military's use of 'yes, sir,' salutes, and other communication that signal status and rank exemplifies which aspect of organizational culture?
   a. Masculine language
   b. Rites
   c. Rituals
   d. Hierarchal vocabulary

4. Every week members of one organization have a collective lunch of pizza and soft drinks. This is an example of a(n):
   a. Task ritual
   b. Personal ritual
   c. Social ritual
   d. Rite of transgression

5. Structures that express and uphold organizational culture includes all BUT ONE of the following.
   a. Roles
   b. Teams
   c. Policies
   d. Rules

6. The two essential features that typify an organization are:
   a. External links and stories
   b. Structure and network
   c. Structure and language

d. Corporate hierarchy and interpersonal channels

7. For Jewish males reaching the age of thirteen, the Bar Mitzvah is a:
   a. Ritual
   b. Cultural role
   c. Habit
   d. Rite

8. A job description for a faculty opening includes the following details: 'Teach three classes a semester, supervise graduate thesis, conduct research, Ph.D. required.' This description is an example of organizational:
   a. Rules
   b. Policies
   c. Stipulations
   d. Roles

9. Among the reasons why we see a rise in romantic relationships between people who work together is:
   a. Because of proximity; more women are working
   b. Because of changing social mores; it has become acceptable
   c. Because of the emancipation of women; more women take the initiative
   d. Because of the lessening of professional standards; no longer prohibited

10. The marked drop off in the travel industry in the United States following the events of September 11, 2001 is a demonstrative example that organizations:
    a. Are highly structured
    b. Are inevitably linked to the external environment
    c. Are internally vulnerable
    d. Are too inflexible

True/False

_____1. Organizations can be understood simply by looking within its operations.
_____2. Organizations are structured.
_____3. Research shows that informal networks of communication (the grapevine) have a very low rate of accuracy.

Identification

1._____ _____ are narratives that convey values, style and the history of an organization.

2.A _____ is especially active during times of organizational change.

3._____ systematize relationships and interactions between members of an.

Essays

1. Explore the concept of organizational culture and consider how it impacts the meanings, traditions and identity of an organization.

2. Compare and contrast formal and informal communication networks in organizations. What is the function of each? What is the reliability of each?

Self-Test for Chapter 12
Public Communication

Multiple Choice

1. Public speaking differs from casual conversation which way?
   a. Less direct interaction with the listener
   b. Requires greater knowledge
   c. Requires more planning and preparation
   d. A and C

2. Communication apprehension is anxiety associated with:
   a. Actual communication encounters
   b. Anticipated communication encounters
   c. Lack of adequate preparation
   d. A and B

3. Which delivery style involves little or no preparation?
   a. Impromptu delivery
   b. Extemporaneous delivery
   c. Printed delivery
   d. Mesmerized delivery

4. To reduce communication apprehension individuals can be taught to revise how they think about communication situations and recognize that the problem is not with speaking but irrational beliefs about speaking. This method is called:
   a. Systematic desensitization
   b. Cognitive restructuring
   c. Positive visualization
   d. Skills training

5. Effective public speaking has been described as being like:
   a. Rhetorical flair
   b. Presentational rhetoric
   c. Enlarged conversation
   d. Conversational control

6. Guidelines for selecting a good topic for a speech include:
   a. Choose a topic that you are unfamiliar with
   b. Avoid narrowing the topic
   c. Select a topic appropriate to listeners
   d. B and C

7. Speeches that have the primary goal of increasing listeners' understanding and knowledge are called:
   a. Narrative speeches

    b. Speeches to inform
    c. Speeches to persuade
    d. Speeches to entertain

8. Which of the following is a spatial pattern of organizing a speech?
    a. Comparing phenomena
    b. Repetition with variation
    c. Organizing ideas according to physical relationships
    d. Patterns organized chronologically

9. A concise statement of the main idea of a speech is called a:
    a. Thesis statement
    b. General purpose for a speech
    c. Evidence
    d. Specific purpose of a speech

10. The trustworthiness that listeners grant a speaker as a result of the speaker's title and achievements is called:
    a. Initial credibility
    b. Derived credibility
    c. Terminal credibility
    d. Expert credibility

11. Among the challenges faced by a public speaker is:
    a. To thoroughly memorize the speech
    b. Not adapting the topic to the audience
    c. Not being a very good story teller
    d. All of the above

12. According to Edward Klinzer, chair of the AMA, 'If everyone had an annual physical, we would save more than a half million lives each year.' This is an example of which kind of evidence?
    a. Statistics
    b. Analogy
    c. Detailed example
    d. Quotation

13. Which of the following is NOT a standard part of an introduction to a speech?
    a. Attention device
    b. Thesis statement
    c. Preview of the body
    d. Presentation of supporting evidence

14. Words and sentences that connect ideas in a speech are referred to as:
    a. Tie-lines
    b. Transitions

c. Previews
d. Visualizations

15. Compared to written style, effective oral style:
    a. Uses more simple sentences than written styles
    b. Should be more personal than written
    c. Is more immediate and active than written
    d. All of the above

True/False

_____1. Communication apprehension is common.
_____2. Presenting material to support a speaker's claim is a way to earn credibility.
_____3. Humor does not have to be part of all speeches that aim to entertain.
_____4. Speaking from a manuscript is advisable when a speech must be precise and with no errors.
_____5. The most common delivery style for public speeches is impromptu style.

Essays

1. Explore the three traditional purposes for public speaking and provide an example of each.

2. Compare and contrast the types of evidence available and describe the appropriate uses of each.

3. Define and describe three kinds of credibility. Your essay should explain how each is developed and who determines a speaker's credibility.

Self-Test for Chapter 13
Mass Communication

Multiple Choice

1. The common perception that Shannon Faulkner was the only cadet to withdraw from the Citadel in 1995 is an example of what media effect?
   a. Cultivation
   b. Encapsulation
   c. Agenda setting
   d. Stabilization

2. During the electronic epoch the dominant sense is:
   a. Sight
   b. Hearing
   c. Touch
   d. B and C

3. The tribal epoch was known as which tradition?
   a. Visual
   b. Listen
   c. Touch
   d. Oral

4. The literate epoch allowed people to:
   a. Pass on rituals by forms of entertainment
   b. To communicate without face-to-face interaction
   c. Rely on the spoken word
   d. Develop keen memories

5. McLuhan claimed that the invention of the printing press:
   a. Inaugurated the industrial revolution
   b. Allowed people to engage in many tasks simultaneously
   c. Revived face-to-face interaction
   d. All of the above

6. Among the functions and effects of mass communication are:
   a. Uses and gratification
   b. Agenda setting
   c. Cultivation
   d. All of the above

7. People and groups that control what information gets to consumers of mass communication are called:
   a. Authorities
   b. Experts

c. Gatekeepers

d. Censors

8. Cultivation theory postulates that people who are heavy viewers of television:
   a. Reflect the worldview of television
   b. Use it for many pleasures and gratifications
   c. Behave more violently than those who watch less
   d. All of the above

9. In an effort to present as many stories as possible television news programs:
   a. Have fewer commercials than entertainment programming
   b. Offer little analysis, depth or reflection
   c. Emphasize violence
   d. B and C

10. The belief that the world is a dangerous place full of mean people who cannot be trusted is one of the basic conditions of:
    a. Resonance
    b. Uses and gratification
    c. Mean world syndrome
    d. Media effect

True/False

_____1. McLuhan claimed that the dominant media in society shapes individual and collective life.

_____2. Mass communication grants a hearing and visibility to some points of view while muting others.

_____3. During the literate epoch the aural tradition reigned.

_____4. Radio telephony ushered in the electronic epoch.

_____5. Cultivation is a cumulative process.

Essays

1. Explain the multiple meanings of the phase 'the medium is the message' or massage.

2. Describe and discuss the ways you can become a more thoughtful and responsible mass media consumer.

Self-Test for Chapter 14
Technologies of Communication

Multiple Choice

1. An advantage of written communication is that it:
    a. Leaves a paper trail
    b. Requires little time to prepare
    c. Does not require precision
    d. A and C

2. The facsimile system:
    a. Lacks the advantage of privacy
    b. Protects from misrepresentation by leaving a hard copy
    c. Is an extension of telephone technology
    d. B and C

3. Email:
    a. Lacks the advantage of privacy
    b. Is an extension of telephone technology
    c. Requires the same skills and time in preparation as written communication
    d. All of the above

4. The traditional pattern of having to house all employees of a company in one location has been transformed by:
    a. Avatars
    b. Memoranda
    c. Teleconferencing
    d. Interconnectivity

5. The ability to engage in a number of chores simultaneously is called:
    a. Multitasking
    b. Multiconferencing
    c. Multiplexity
    d. Multilaboring

6. The most notable advantage of computer conferencing is that:
    a. It is linear and requires each participant to await their turn
    b. Is its relative low cost and ability for participants to remain in their work environment
    c. It closely emulates in-person interaction
    d. It is good news for people who are not tech-savvy

7. Among the challenges of our increasing use of newer and newer communication technologies:
    a. Are issues revolving around privacy of information

b. Are issues revolving around more democratic access
c. Are issues revolving around regulation
d. All of the above

8. Which variety of teleconferencing most closely emulates in-person communication?
    a. Computer conferencing
    b. Videoconferencing
    c. Interconferencing
    d. Audioconferencing

9. Virtual communities:
    a. May promote narcissism
    b. Require less commitment and accommodation among members
    c. Allow people the opportunity to falsely represent themselves
    d. All of the above

10. Connecting various devices to each other and to the Internet so that the user doesn't have the hassle of configuring each new system is the meaning of:
    a. Teleconnectivity
    b. Intraconnectivity
    c. Adaptability
    d. Interconnectivity

True/False

_____1. Electronic mail is one of the most popular uses of the Internet.
_____2. We communicate the same with written and computer mediated communication.
_____3. Interconnectivity is conducting meetings with people who are geographically separated.
_____4. Information overload can result from being swamped by the amount of communication and information that demands our attention.
_____5. In online communication, basic aspects of personal identity can easily be fabricated.

Essays

1. Discuss different points of view on the impact of communication technologies on social division. How do scholars believe that the new and converging technologies will affect the gap between the 'haves' and 'have nots'?

2. Describe how new and converging technologies alter (or fail to alter) the meaning of community.

Self-Test for Appendix
Communication in Interviews

Multiple Choice

1. Your doctor asking you a series of questions regarding your recent medical history is an interview that has which purpose?
   a. Giving information
   b. Getting information
   c. Problem solving
   d. Performance review

2. Bill notices that Chris has been making a lot of careless mistakes in his recent work. Bill calls Chris in to discuss the matter. This interview has which of the following purposes?
   a. Counseling
   b. Performance review
   c. Reprimand
   d. Exit

3. Interviews that are designed to create anxiety in interviewees are called:
   a. Tension exchanges
   b. Argumentative interviews
   c. Stress interviews
   d. Authoritarian interviews

4. The interview style in which the interviewee has the greatest potential to control content and pace is the:
   a. Distributive interview
   b. Mirror interview
   c. Tension interviews
   d. Authoritarian interview

5. 'So, what can you tell me about yourself?' This is which of the following types of question?
   a. Open
   b. Closed
   c. Probing
   d. Leading

6. Which style of interviewing has the greatest imbalance of power between interviewer and interviewee?
   a. Mirror
   b. Closed
   c. Probing
   d. Stress

7. 'You wouldn't mind traveling, would you?' This is which of the following types of question?
   a. Open
   b. Closed
   c. Distributive
   d. Leading

8. 'What would you do if a person you were supervising was continually late for work?' is what kind of question?
   a. Hypothetical
   b. Problem solving
   c. Probing
   d. Leading

9. Questions that are illegal in most contexts can be asked if they pertain to:
   a. The company's culture
   b. Bona fide job qualifications
   c. The interviewer's personal values
   d. The interviewer's religious commitments

10. The stage of the interviewing process which usually consumes the bulk of the interview time is the:
    a. Exit stage
    b. Substantive stage
    c. Closing stage
    d. Hypothetical stage

True/False

_____1. EEOC regulations prohibit discrimination on the basis of criteria that are irrelevant to job qualifications.

_____2. Interviewers have the greatest control over interview content and pace in mirror interviews.

_____3. Persuasive interviews are used to collaboratively solve problems.

_____4. Interviews are a common form of communication for many people.

_____5. The opening stage of an interview should establish an effective climate.

Essays

1. Define the funnel sequence in interviewing. Explain how it operates and provide a concrete example of the funnel sequence.

2. What can interviewees do to prepare for effective participation in employment interviews? Be specific and use examples in your response.

ANSWERS TO SELF-TEST QUESTIONS

Chapter 1

Multiple Choice

1. B
2. B
3. B
4. D
5. C
6. B
7. C
8. C
9. C
10. A

True/False

1. False
2. True
3. False
4. False
5. True

Chapter 2

Multiple Choice

1. C
2. B
3. A
4. B
5. C
6. A
7. D
8. A
9. C
10. C

True/False

1. False
2. False
3. False
4. True
5. False

Chapter 3

Multiple Choice

1. D
2. B
3. A
4. D
5. A
6. C
7. B
8. A
9. C
10. A

True/False

1. False
2. False
3. True
4. False
5. True

Chapter 4

Multiple Choice

1. D
2. A
3. B
4. A
5. C
6. B
7. C
8. A
9. C
10. A

True/False

1. False
2. False
3. True
4. True
5. False

Chapter 5

Multiple Choice

1. C
2. B
3. C
4. B
5. D
6. C
7. A
8. C
9. B
10. C

True/False

1. True
2. True
3. True
4. False
5. True

Chapter 6

Multiple Choice

1. C
2. D
3. A
4. D
5. C
6. B
7. A
8. B
9. A
10. C

True/False

1. False
2. False
3. True
4. True
5. False

Chapter 5

Multiple Choice

1. C
2. B
3. C
4. B
5. D
6. C
7. A
8. C
9. B
10. C

True/False

1. True
2. True
3. True
4. False
5. True

Chapter 6

Multiple Choice

1. C
2. D
3. A
4. D
5. C
6. B
7. A
8. B
9. A
10. C

True/False

1. False
2. False
3. True
4. True
5. False

Chapter 7

Multiple Choice

1. B
2. D
3. A
4. C
5. D
6. A
7. B
8. B
9. D
10. B

True/False

1. False
2. False
3. True
4. True
5. True

Chapter 8

Multiple Choice

1. C
2. D
3. C
4. A
5. A
6. C
7. B
8. C
9. D
10. C

True/False

1. False
2. True
3. False
4. True
5. False

Chapter 9

Multiple Choice

1. B
2. B
3. A
4. C
5. B
6. B
7. D
8. A
9. D
10. C

True/False

1. False
2. False
3. False
4. True
5. True

Chapter 10

Multiple Choice

1. B
2. D
3. A
4. D
5. B
6. C
7. D
8. A
9. B
10. B

True/False

1. False
2. True
3. True
4. True
5. False

Chapter 11

Multiple Choice

1. A
2. C
3. D
4. C
5. B
6. B
7. D
8. D
9. A
10. B

True/False

1. False
2. True
3. False
4. True
5. False

Identification

1. Corporate stories
2. Grapevine
3. Structures

Chapter 12

Multiple Choice

1. D
2. D
3. A
4. B
5. C
6. C
7. B
8. C
9. A
10. A
11. B
12. A
13. D
14. B
15. D

True/False

1. True
2. False
3. True
4. False
5. True

Chapter 13

Multiple Choice

1. C
2. D
3. D
4. B
5. A
6. D
7. C
8. A
9. D
10. C

True/False

1. True
2. True
3. False
4. False
5. True

Chapter 14

Multiple Choice

1. A
2. D
3. A
4. C
5. A
6. B
7. D
8. B
9. D
10. D

True/False

1. True
2. False
3. False
4. True
5. True

Appendix

Multiple Choice

1. B
2. C
3. C
4. B
5. A
6. D
7. D
8. A
9. B
10. B

True/False

1. True
2. False
3. False
4. True
5. True